THE
ACCIDENTAL
DICTIONARY

THE
ACCIDENTAL
DICTIONARY

The Remarkable Twists and
Turns of English Words

PAUL ANTHONY JONES

PEGASUS BOOKS
NEW YORK LONDON

THE ACCIDENTAL DICTIONARY

Pegasus Books Ltd
148 West 37th Street, 13th Floor
New York, NY 10018

ISBN: 978-1-68177-569-2

10 9 8 7 6 5 4 3 2 1

Printed in the United States of America
Distributed by W. W. Norton & Company, Inc.

For Nick, Chris and Gav

CONTENTS

INTRODUCTION

One of the enduringly great things about language is that it is in a continuous state of change. The words we use every day are relentlessly evolving and shape-shifting, broadening and specialising, adjusting and reworking themselves from one decade to the next.

At times, these changes can seem fairly predictable. Take a word like *computer*, for instance. Derived from the verb *compute* (which in turn has its roots in a Latin word meaning 'to reckon'), when it first emerged in the early 1600s it referred, quite literally, to someone employed in performing computations and calculations. But as technology progressed, so too did the word. By the turn of the nineteenth century a *computer* was a mechanical device used to perform or assist in performing complex calculations, and from there the first reference to an electronic computer emerged in 1946.

Not all etymological stories are quite so straightforward, however. Delving into the histories of the words we know and use every day can often reveal some fairly peculiar developments, as the routes they take through the language are not always so smooth and uneventful. Instead words are knocked and buffeted, subjected to twists and turns, expansions and contractions, happy and unhappy accidents, at the end of which they can find themselves far removed from their starting points.

Take the word *accident* itself. It derives from a Latin root meaning 'to fall', and so when it first appeared in the language in the fourteenth century referred merely to any event or occurrence. Put another way, an *accident* was originally an incident. Within a hundred years or so, however, that sense had narrowed so that an *accident* was now a chance event, either good or bad, that had occurred unexpectedly or unintentionally, or without prior knowledge or interference. And finally from there – and perhaps because bad luck always seems to make more of a talking point than good luck – that meaning narrowed again, so that by the late 1500s *accident* had become a byword for a specifically unfortunate event or a mishap, the sense in which it finds itself chiefly in use today. All in all, *accident* has been on quite the accidental journey – and it's by no means alone.

Cast an etymological eye over the other words in your vocabulary and you soon see even more unanticipated tales emerge. *Girls*, you discover, could once be boys. Your *nephew* was originally your grandson. The *queen* was your wife. A *shampoo* was a massage. *Clouds* were rocks. *Noon* was 3pm. Once upon a time, you could eat *potpourri*. You could paint with *pencils*, get *drenched* in a *tiddlywink*, fall for a *hat-trick*, and end the night looking utterly *raunchy*. Under scrutiny, the dictionary reveals an unpredictable network of etymological crossed paths, U-turns and forks-in-the-road like these, mapped out as its words dart from one meaning to another over centuries of development. It becomes an accidental dictionary.

The Accidental Dictionary

Affiliate

originally meant 'to adopt a child'

Affiliate is a word whose etymological journey has taken it from rather humble and straightforward beginnings in the early 1600s, through to the ultra-modern worlds of e-commerce and online marketing. A typical twenty-first-century glossary of business-speak or internet jargon – full of the kinds of words that once you learn their meaning, you really wish you hadn't – will include entries for *affiliate networks*, *affiliate trackers* and *affiliate aggregators*. Websites will send you *affiliate links*. Internet marketing aficionados (more on those in a moment) will talk of *affiliate cloaking*. Online companies will sign *affiliation agreements*. It's all absolutely riveting.

That hasn't always been the case of course – the word *affiliate* is four centuries old, after all. But even in these jargonish contemporary applications, the word's basic meaning survives: as a verb, *affiliate* means 'to connect', 'to join' or 'to cooperate with', while as a noun it's a synonym of words such as *associate*, *colleague* and *partner*. Either way, it's clearly concerned with association and incorporation, partnership and community. Keeping things in a family, you could say – which is, in fact, precisely what it once meant.

At the centre of the word *affiliate* is the Latin word for

'son', *filius*, an etymological root that it shares with the likes of *filial* and *filicide*, as well as a host of superbly obscure words such as *filionymic* ('a name derived from that of your son') and *filiopietism* ('excessive veneration of your ancestors'). When it first appeared in the language in the early seventeenth century, *affiliate* meant 'to adopt a child' – or, as the English lexicographer Henry Cockeram defined it in his brilliantly titled *English Dictionarie, or an Interpreter of Hard English Words* (1623), 'to choose one for his son'.

This original meaning steadily developed so that by the mid 1700s *affiliate* had come to be used to mean 'to ascertain the parenthood of a child' – making *affiliation* essentially eighteenth-century legalese for a paternity test. As one London newspaper reported in 1798, an appropriately named 'Mr Law' had recently appeared in court with 'an affidavit which stated that Mary Walker came to him in order to affiliate a bastard child', while an 1842 digest of legal cases on the Isle of Man declared that:

> By the common law of the Isle of Man . . . a widow is entitled to dower only *'dum sola et casta vixerit'* [*'as long as she stays unmarried and chaste'*], and was held to have forfeited it by the birth and affiliation of a bastard child.

Blimey, they really didn't mince their words back then.

Although uncommon, this legal use of *affiliate* still survives today, but it is the broader, more generalised use of *affiliate* to mean merely 'to connect to' or 'to become associated with' – a figurative development that first emerged in the mid 1700s – that has since established itself the word's most familiar meaning.

Aficionado

originally meant 'amateur'

If all that talk of *affiliate aggregators* and *affiliation agreements* leaves you clueless, you could always turn to an online *aficionado* to help you out. That's because an *aficionado* is an expert, right? A connoisseur. A die-hard follower. Someone who knows so much about a certain subject that they're the go-to authority on it. Well, that might be the case today, but originally things were quite different.

Take this line from a letter written in 1797 by a German travel writer named Frederick Augustus Fischer, after he had attended a bullfight in Bilbao, Spain:

> At each end of the square an amphitheatre was erected, and the whole enclosed with palisades. The benches

and balconies on either side bent under the weight of the spectators . . . the square itself was a crowd of aficionados or amateurs, who came there to be active in striking the bulls, but so as to escape in case of need by leaping over the palisades.

Frankly, if an enraged bull were running towards you then leaping out of the amphitheatre might be a better idea than 'leaping over the palisades'. But improvised escape routes aside, there is an odd juxtaposition of words here: how does 'a crowd of aficionados or amateurs' make sense? Surely if you're an *aficionado*, you're no longer an amateur?

It will come as little surprise to find that *aficionado* was borrowed into English from Spanish, a little over 200 years ago – in fact, the 1802 English edition of Fischer's *Travels in Spain* gives us our earliest written record of it. But in its native Spanish, the word dates back to the fifteenth century and has its origins in an even older word, *afición*, meaning 'affection', 'fondness' or 'inclination'. That made an *aficionado* originally just an enthusiast – namely someone who enjoyed or supported, or else had a fondness for or an interest in, some particular pursuit, pastime or philosophy. But if you really enjoy something, it might be only a matter of time before you decide to try it out for yourself.

That might not include bullfighting, admittedly, but the *aficionados* mentioned by Fischer had nevertheless turned up ringside to try their hand at a little tauromachy, and take pot-shots at the luckless bulls in the bullring. Through association with them, the word *aficionado* soon came to refer to what we might now call an amateur practitioner or a dabbler, and in that sense became particularly attached to bullfighting: by the mid 1600s, it was being used in its native Spanish to refer specifically to an amateur bullfighter, and it was this meaning that was imported into English, via Fischer's travelogue, in the early 1800s.

But, as the saying goes, practice makes perfect. Try your hand at something, perhaps even bullfighting, for long enough and you will soon see yourself improving. Consequently, by the mid nineteenth century *aficionado* had begun to be used to refer to any ardent, experienced and knowledgeable devotee or fanatic, regardless of the discipline involved. And it is that meaning, rather than the original, that has survived through to English today.

Album

originally meant 'a blank stone tablet'

Imagine pressing play on your favourite album and hearing nothing. Total silence. Unless you're a John Cage fan, the chances are that there would be something amiss. But etymologically, it would make perfect sense.

Album is a derivative of the Latin word for 'white', *albus*. That's also where the *albumen* of an egg takes its name, as well as *albinism*, a priest's *alb*, and the *albedo* or quantity of light reflected by a surface. It's also, somewhat confusingly, where the word *auburn* originated, long before it lost the L and, thanks to three centuries of being spelled *aborne*, became confused with the colour *brown*.

But back to albums. In Ancient Rome, the Latin word *album* was used to refer to a blank stone tablet or board, either naturally white or painted white, on which important edicts and other publicly significant records such as lists of magistrates or the events of the year would be written. In this sense, it was particularly associated with the highest of the high priests, the *pontifex maximus*, who would display his personal records, or *annales maximi*, on a series of 'albums' outside his home.

But when the Roman Empire collapsed, it took the word *album* with it. It languished in one of the dustier corners of the dictionary for more than a thousand years, until a curious trend emerged in mid-sixteenth-century Europe: in an otherwise blank notebook known as an *album amicorum* or 'book of friends', German scholars and academics began collecting their colleagues' signatures, often with quips and witty epigrams written alongside them. It was the trend for these autograph books that first brought the word *album* to the attention of the English language in the early 1600s, when it initially referred only to a blank jotter or notebook used to collect odd lines of text and other literary miscellanea – or, as Samuel Johnson defined it in his *Dictionary of the English Language* (1755), 'a book in which foreigners have long been accustomed to insert autographs of celebrated people'.

This meaning broadened over time, so that by the mid 1800s the word *album* was being used to refer to any large-leaved scrapbook or folder used to display keepsakes and souvenirs such as photographs, stamps and postcards. As for musical albums, when the first gramophone records began to appear in the early 1900s, they were packaged in protective sleeves resembling the broad pages of these Victorian picture albums, and while you're more likely to download an album than hold one in your hands these days, the word has remained in use ever since.

Alcohol

originally meant 'eye shadow'

There aren't many etymological stories that begin with the sublimation of a crystalline sulphite mineral, but there is at least one. It just happens also to be the story behind one of the most familiar words in the English language. So brace yourself — here comes the science bit.

When a substance changes directly from a solid into a gas with no intermediate liquid phase, that's sublimation. It's the same process that turns dry ice into a thick white fog without leaving pools of liquid carbon dioxide everywhere, but that's not to suggest that sublimation is all about cheap special effects. Back in Ancient Egypt, the mineral stibnite was heated to produce, via sublimation, a fine smoky vapour that left a layer of sooty powder on any surface with which it came into contact. The Egyptians then collected this powder (antimony trisulphide, should you really want to know) and mixed it with animal grease to produce a thick black paste that could be then used as a kind of eye shadow. Different colours could be made by crushing, grinding or sublimating different chemicals — galena, an ore of lead, produced a rich grey colour, while malachite produced a dark green — but whatever the raw ingredients, the name of this cosmetic paste was always the same: *kohl*, a term derived from an ancient Arabic word meaning 'stain' or 'paint'.

Now here comes the language bit. In Arabic, the definite article, 'the', is a prefix, *al–*. That's the same *al–* found in names like *Algeria* ('the islands'), *Allah* ('the god'), and *Alhambra* ('the red castle'), as well as words such as *alkali* ('the ashes'), *almanac* ('the calendar') and *algebra* (more on that in a moment), and it also gave the Ancient Egyptians' eye shadow the name *al-kohl*. The chemists and alchemists of the Middle Ages then stumbled across this term in their ancient textbooks, and began applying it to any fine powder produced by sublimation – and it is in this sense that the word *alcohol* first appeared in English in the mid 1500s.

But to all those chemists and alchemists, sublimation was more than just a way of accentuating your eyes. Instead, it was a way of extracting the purest, most absolute essence of something, and it wasn't long before they began applying the same techniques and ideas – not to mention the same word – to liquids.

The concentrated, intensified liquors that could be produced by refining and distilling fluids ultimately came to be known as *alcohol* as well, and because one of the fluids these early experiments were carried out on happened to be wine, by the mid nineteenth century the term had become particularly associated with so-called 'alcohol of wine' – namely the alcoholic content of intoxicating liquor. Eventually, this meaning, and its associations with alcoholic spirits and beverages, established itself as the way in which the word was most widely used, while its ancient associations with sublimation and Egyptian cosmetics dropped into relative obscurity.

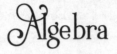 Algebra

originally meant 'bone-setting surgery'

If you didn't much care for mathematics at school, it might come as little surprise to learn that *algebra* started out as another word for the agonising bone-setting surgery used to heal fractures — which frankly might sound like a more enjoyable way to spend your time than working your way through the likes of $ax^2 + bx + c = 0$.

Algebra is a Latin corruption of the Arabic *al-jabr*, literally meaning 'the reunion' or 'the restoration' of something lost or broken — it just so happens that the things being 'reunited' or 'restored' were originally broken bones, not unknown quantities. It was in this sense, as a medical term referring to the healing and treatment of fractures, that the word *algebra* was first imported into English in the early Middle Ages via translations of European and Arabic medical textbooks:

as one English translation of *La Grande Chirurgerie* or 'The Grand Surgery' (*c.* 1425) put it, *algebra* was originally the 'stretching out and/or restoring of broken bones and bones out of joint'. That would have been that too, were it not for the arrival of a ninth-century Persian mathematician called Muḥammad ibn Mūsā al-Khwārizmī.

In 830 AD, al-Khwārizmī wrote a mathematical treatise called *The Concise Book on Calculation by Restoration and Completion*, in which the things being 'restored' by *al-jabr* were no longer broken bones, but the unknown quantities in quadratic equations. By figuratively referring to these kinds of calculations as *al-jabr*, al-Khwārizmī laid the foundations not only for the word *algebra*, but the entire discipline of algebra itself (as well as countless hours of bewildering mathematics lessons). This arithmetical meaning of *algebra* arrived in English in the mid 1500s, and the subject's widespread popularity soon helped to consign the older medical use of *algebra* to the history books.

Al-Khwārizmī's work, however, wasn't done. With a little linguistic twisting and turning, his surname eventually morphed into the title of another branch of mathematics that his work helped to introduce: *algorithms*. If you don't like maths, you really have only one person to blame . . .

Ambidextrous

originally meant 'duplicitous'

The first six letters of the word *ambidextrous* come from the first half of the alphabet, while the last six letters come from the second half. That has absolutely no bearing on the history of the word itself, of course, it's just a nice bit of trivia. Speaking of which, James A. Garfield, the twentieth President of the United States, reportedly had an astonishing party piece: having solicited a question from his friends or fellow party guests, he would write the answer in Latin with one hand and, simultaneously, in Ancient Greek with the other. Besides being clearly a very proficient classicist, Garfield is credited with being the first *ambidextrous* president — and would have been the last, had Gerald Ford not once claimed to be 'left-handed sitting down and right-handed standing up'.

Apologies to all southpaws, but the word *ambidextrous* literally means 'right-handed on both sides' (while its seldom-used opposite *ambilaevous* literally means 'left-handed on both sides'). So what we really mean by calling President Garfield *ambidextrous* is that he was able to use his left hand as proficiently as his right. That might be the literal meaning of *ambidextrous*, however, but it was by no means the first.

When it originally emerged in the language back in

the sixteenth century, *ambidextrous* meant 'deceitful' or 'double-dealing', while an *ambidexter* was a dishonest lawyer or juror who would accept a payment (literally, one in each hand) from both parties in a legal dispute. The more familiar use of *ambidextrous* to mean 'capable of using both hands equally well' emerged much later in the 1500s. For a while, these two meanings – one carrying connotations of duplicity and double-dealing, the other dexterity and intelligence – coexisted in the language until the current meaning finally took precedence in the early nineteenth century. Today, it remains the only meaning of *ambidextrous* still in widespread use.

Archipelago

was originally another name for the Aegean Sea

The Aegean Sea between Greece and Turkey is traditionally said to take its name from the Athenian king Aegeus, who drowned himself in its waters after he wrongly presumed that his son Theseus (more on him later) had been killed. The earliest description of the Aegean in English comes from a sixteenth-century encyclopaedic chronicle called *The Customs of London* (1503), which described 'the west quarter of the world', as extending as far as 'Corfu . . . and many other isles within the archipelago that is the gulf between Greece and Turkey'. But the *archipelago* mentioned here is not the mass of islands strewn across the Aegean Sea – it's the Aegean Sea itself.

The word *archipelago* combines the Greek words *archos*, meaning 'chief' or 'ruler' (as in *archangel* and *archbishop*) and *pelagos*, meaning 'sea'. Together, that makes an *archipelago* literally a 'chief sea', and as there was no stretch of water more important to the Ancient Greeks than the Aegean, the word *archipelago* simply began life as another name for it. If you know your geography, however, you'll know the Aegean Sea is absolutely full of islands. Well, perhaps not full, because then there'd be no water. But from Adelfoi Islets to the tiny rocky outcrop of Zourafa, the Aegean is home to more than 2,500 islands – and the explorers and geographers of the sixteenth century knew it.

Thanks to its island-studded appearance on maps and navigational charts, during the Age of Exploration the Aegean's alternative name, *archipelago*, came to be used as a byword for any newly discovered patch of ocean that appeared equally crowded with islands. Hence when the English explorer Martin Frobisher arrived in the island-strewn Canadian Arctic in 1578, he noted:

These broken landes and ilandes, being very many in number, do seeme to make there an Archipelagus,

which as they all differ in greatnesse, forme, and
fashion, one from another, so are they in goodnesse,
couloure, and soyle muche unlike.

— George Best, *A True Discourse of
the Late Voyages of Discovery* (1578)

By the time that the Aegean Sea's existing name came to be
more widely known in the early 1600s, however, things had
changed. The word *archipelago* was no longer being used of
island-strewn patches of water, but of the islands themselves
— as in this description of the Moluccas or Indonesian Spice
Islands by the Portuguese explorer Fernão Mendes Pinto:

For then he might have means, with less charge, to shut
up the Straights of Cincapura *[Singapore]* . . . and so stop
our Ships from passing to the Seas of China . . . and
the Molucques; whereby he might have the profit of
all the Drugs which came from that great Archipelague.

— Henry Cogan (trans.), *The Voyages
and Adventures of Ferdinand Mendez Pinto* (1663)

Pinto's account was translated into English in 1663, and
the meaning of *archipelago* has remained unchanged ever since.

Bank

originally meant 'table'

The 'banks' found in words like *riverbank, sandbank, cloudbank* and *embankment* are, etymologically at least, the same. They all have a common ancestor in an old Scandinavian word meaning 'hill' or 'mound', whose modern-day equivalents still survive in other northern European languages such as Swedish (*bank*), Finnish (*penkka*) and Icelandic (*bakki*). The 'bank' found in monetary words like *banker, banknote, bankroll* and *piggybank*, however, is different. It arrived in English via French in the fifteenth century, and although it probably descends from the same ancient Germanic root as all those other *banks*, its origins lie in Renaissance Italy and the Italian word for a bench or table, *banca*. But how did a table come to mean a bank?

In the early Middle Ages, grain merchants in Italy began lending money to their suppliers to cover the costs of planting, cultivating and harvesting their crops. As time went by, this business of lending money soon proved more profitable an enterprise than the grain trade itself, which led some merchants to abandon agriculture altogether and establish their own money-lending ventures. They still operated their business from where they always had, however, at a stall in the local marketplace: sitting behind nothing more than a low wooden table or *banca*, these early merchant bankers not only established the practice of modern banking, but gave us the word *bank* itself.

Where there's money to be made, of course, there's money to be lost. Some of these early moneylenders started to offer insurance for traders who were unsure of the success of their crops or reliability of their supply routes, while others expanded their businesses beyond merely financing their own suppliers and began holding deposits for other traders whose deals were still being thrashed out. In the meantime, the cash obtained from these deposits and insurances could be loaned out to other merchants and suppliers – but there was never any guarantee that these investments were sound. A moneylender who lost his traders' cash or deposits in bad investments would ultimately have to face an understandably angry crowd of ruined customers, who would symbolically smash his table to pieces – and it's from the Italian *banca rotta*, or 'broken bench', that we eventually took the word *bankrupt*. Frankly, it all gives a whole new meaning to a banker's crash.

Bimbo

was originally a man

All the words so far on this list have certainly changed their meanings, but *bimbo* is the first to have changed its gender. Derived from an Italian word for a baby boy (a baby girl would be a *bimba*), when it first emerged in American slang in the early 1900s, *bimbo* was used both of an unimportant or insignificant man, and a menacing, brutish dolt or bully. It's been suggested that the word might have entered the American vernacular through songs or stage shows performed by Italian immigrants, but in truth no one is entirely sure how or why it came to be adopted into English. One thing that is clear, however, is that it was originally an exclusively masculine insult – although it didn't take long for all that to change.

In 1920, American songwriters Grant Clarke and Walter Donaldson collaborated on a song called *My Little Bimbo Down on the Bamboo Isle*. Written for a Broadway revue called *Silks and Satins*, the song described a 'handsome sailor boy' who fell for a beautiful native girl 'on a Fiji-iji Isle . . . beneath a bamboo tree'. Although the lyrics don't give away too many etymological clues ('I don't know what "bimbo" means / But I think it's something nice', goes the not-too-insightful final verse), it is nevertheless clear that the song is being far from derogatory about the girl in question. The song's portrayal of a *bimbo* as little more than a beautiful, voluptuous woman, however, soon led to the word being associated with empty-headedness, vacuousness and eventually promiscuity. Consequently, a 'primer of Broadway slang' that appeared in a 1927 edition of *Vanity Fair* defined a *bimbo* as 'a dumb girl', while in *The Broadway Melody* (1929) – the first talkie to win Best Picture at the Oscars – no-nonsense stage dancer Hank Mahoney memorably threatens another actress with the line, 'One more crack from you, bimbo, and you'll be holding a lily!'

For a time, both the male and female versions of the *bimbo* co-existed; P. G. Wodehouse was still using *bimbo* to refer to a man as late as the 1940s, writing of 'bimbos who went about the place making passes at innocent girls after discarding their wives like old tubes of toothpaste' in his comic novel *Full Moon* (1947). But by the later twentieth century the male version had all but vanished, thanks largely to a number of high-profile scandals involving beautiful young women and older businessmen (which led to the *Wall Street Journal* famously dubbing 1987 'The Year of the Bimbo'). In fact, by the late 1980s the word had become so exclusively female that a male equivalent had to be reinvented – the earliest record of the *himbo* dates from 1988.

Blockbuster

was originally a bomb

These days, when a film fails to earn its money back at the box office, it bombs. But when a film turns out to be a *blockbuster* success, it is still literally a 'bomb' – and the reason why takes us back to wartime Great Britain.

At the height of the Second World War, the Royal Air Force began developing a new design for an enormous aerial bomb designated the 'high-capacity' or HC bomb. Built with a thinner-than-normal outer casing, intended to leave as much room inside as possible for explosive material, the HCs were designed to be larger and more powerful than any other bomb yet employed by the British military. After months of development, the first HC emerged in 1941: 9 foot long and made of half a ton of steel, it weighed a total of 4,000 pounds, a staggering three-quarters of which was pure explosive Amatol.

On 31 March 1941, the first of these 4,000-pound bombs was dropped in a raid on the city of Emden in north-west Germany – one of the pilots involved in the raid later described how 'whole houses took to the air' – but as the war intensified, the RAF continued to produce larger and ever more powerful HCs. In 1942, an 8,000-pound bomb was developed, followed the next year by a 12,000-pound bomb, which was first used in a devastating attack on the Dortmund–Ems Canal on 15 September 1943. By the end of the war, more than 120,000 HCs had been dropped on German targets, containing between them a total of a quarter of a million tons of explosive material.

To Britain's RAF pilots, these enormous bombs were unassumingly nicknamed 'cookies'. To the Germans, they were the *Bezirkbomben*, or 'district bombs'. And to the English-speaking press, they were *blockbusters* – bombs so extraordinarily powerful that they could literally destroy an entire block of buildings:

> Berlin was attacked by an all-Lancaster force that had to battle through ice and cloud to the hidden target . . . As the 'block-busters' fell, fires glowed over a wide area. Series of violent explosions burst through the clouds even when the bomb flashes were hidden.
> – *Daily Mail*, 20 November 1943

The name *blockbuster* is actually thought to have been coined by American war reporters, but its use quickly caught on elsewhere. By the mid 1940s, it was not only being used by British journalists, but had slipped into wider use and soon anything of great size, impact, success or significance – from political speeches to Broadway stage shows to bestselling novels

— was being labelled a *blockbuster*. The word's military connotations understandably dwindled after the war, and finally this figurative meaning took its place permanently in the language.

Brothel

originally meant 'a good-for-nothing'

In Shakespeare's *King Lear*, one of the king's ungrateful daughters, Goneril, laments how the king's court has degenerated into 'more like a tavern or brothel than a graced palace'. In his *Dictionary of the English Language* (1755), Samuel Johnson somewhat euphemistically defined a *brothel* as 'a house of lewd entertainment'. And when the Puritan preacher Henry Smith delivered a typically fire-and-brimstone sermon under the title of 'Satan's Compassing the Earth' in 1593, he exclaimed:

> I do verily think that some here did come from as bad exercises as the Devil himself; and that when they do depart from this place, they will return to as bad exercises again as the Devil did; some unto the taverns, some unto the alehouses, and some unto the stages, and some unto the brothels.

Aside from the fact that Smith clearly saw acting as just as opprobrious a pursuit as drinking and whore-mongering, it is clear from his quote, and the others here, that a *brothel* has long been used as a word for a house of ill repute – but that hasn't always been the case.

Brothel is derived from an Old English word, *breoðen*, which essentially meant 'deteriorated', 'degenerate' or 'gone to ruin'. From that emerged a Middle English word, *broþel*, which was used to refer not to a ruined or dilapidated building, but rather to a ruined or degenerate man, a scoundrel or a good-for-nothing – or, as the *Oxford English Dictionary* eloquently puts it, 'a worthless, abandoned fellow'. This was the only meaning of the word *brothel* in use for much of the early Middle Ages; it appears in several principal works of medieval literature, and is even used in the script of one of the York mystery plays (*c.* 1440) in reference to Jesus Christ. But just because *brothel* didn't mean back then what it does today, doesn't mean that there wasn't a word for 'a house of lewd entertainment' in the Middle Ages. After all, we are talking about the world's oldest profession.

What we might now call a *brothel* was originally a *bordel*, a French-origin word borrowed into English in the thirteenth century that literally means 'cabin' or 'hut' (and is, appropriately enough, the origin of the word *bordello*). By the late fifteenth century, however, the two words had become confused: *brothel* was now being used to refer to fallen women as well as good-for-nothing men, and ultimately *bordels* came to be known as *brothel-houses* in the early 1500s. All it took from there was for the word 'house' to be dropped, and the transformation of *brothel* from 'wretch' or 'scoundrel' to Samuel Johnson's 'house of lewd entertainment' was finally complete.

Bumph

originally meant 'toilet paper'

There is really no nice way of putting this: the word *bumph* began life as nineteenth-century slang for toilet paper, but can trace its origins way back to a Middle English word for a bundle of grass used to wipe your backside. This wholly unlikely story begins in an even more unlikely way, with the *Promptorium Parvulorum* or 'Storehouse for Children' (*c.* 1440), the first bilingual Latin dictionary ever published in English. Compiled by a Norfolk-born monk known as Geoffrey the Grammarian, among the hundreds of entries translated in this linguistic 'storehouse' was the Middle English word *arswyspe*, for which Geoffrey helpfully offered two Latin translations: *memperium* and *anitergium*.

In not too uncertain terms, *arswyspe* was essentially poor-man's toilet paper in medieval England – it literally refers to a 'wisp' or tuft of grass or straw used to clean your 'arse'. *Memperium* meanwhile is thought to combine the Latin words for 'hand' (*manus*) and 'purify' (*piare*), and so literally means something like 'hand-held cleanser'. And *anitergium* is the least understated of the three, as it literally means 'anus-wiper' (and comes from the same root as the word *detergent*). But brace yourselves – we're not done yet.

Replace the *arse* and *wisp* in Geoffrey's *arswyspe* with synonyms for a person's buttocks and a pile of dry grass, and you'll end up at *bum-fodder*, a word that first emerged as another name for toilet paper in a 1653 translation of *Gargantua* (1534), a work by the French novelist Rabelais. Chapter 13 of *Gargantua* comprises a long conversation between the title character, a giant and his equally enormous father, Grangousier, who are talking about all the things that can be used to wipe your behind – and nothing, according to Grangousier, comes close to a goose's neck:

I wiped my tail with a hen, with a cock, with a pullet, with a calf's skin, with a hare, with a pigeon, with a cormorant, with an attorney's bag, with a montero [*a Spanish hunter's cap*], with a coif [*a nightcap*], with a falconer's lure. But, to conclude, I say and maintain, that of all torcheculs, arsewisps, bumfodders, tail-napkins, bunghole cleansers, and wipe-breeches, there is none in the world comparable to the neck of a goose that is well downed, if you hold her head betwixt your legs.

Subtlety may not exactly have been Rabelais' forte, but it was nevertheless this bizarre paragraph that first introduced the word *bum-fodder* to the English language in the mid 1600s. By the eighteenth century, its use had broadened, so that *bum-fodder* was now being used as a comical nickname for trashy, throwaway literature. The clipped form *bumf* or *bumph* then emerged in the late nineteenth century, both as schoolyard slang for paper (one 1898 *Dictionary of Slang, Jargon and Cant* even defined a *bumf-hunt* as 'a paper-chase') and as a humorous nickname for toilet paper. And from there, *bumph* finally came to be used as a metaphor for any tedious, worthless or unnecessarily wordy document or piece of text, and it's this meaning alone that has survived through to English today.

Busking

was originally piracy

There is an old etymological myth that claims that *busking*, in the sense of giving some kind of public performance for cash, derives from *buskin*, a sixteenth-century word for a type of knee-length leather boot once popular among actors and itinerant players. Indeed *to wear the buskins* meant 'to perform or write a drama', or 'to act tragically or melodramatically' in eighteenth-century English. It's certainly a nice idea, but sadly not one word of it is true – and, with apologies to all buskers, the true story behind *busking* is potentially a lot less complimentary.

The verb *busk* first emerged in the English language in the early 1600s. Its earliest meaning is thought to have been a nautical one: *busking* originally meant 'sailing a ship to and fro' or 'sailing a zigzagging course', especially if by doing so the ship managed to 'beat to windward' (i.e. made good headway against a strong prevailing wind). In this sense, it's thought that *busk* was borrowed into English from its Spanish equivalent, *buscar*, but probably has its roots in an even earlier French word, *busquer*, which meant merely 'to seek' or 'to search'.

You'd be forgiven for thinking that all this sounds perfectly *above board* (which despite appearances is not another naval expression, but alludes to honest card players keeping their hands above the table). But, alas, there's a problem. As well as meaning merely 'to seek' in French, the verb *busquer* was also used to mean 'to prowl', 'to catch', 'to scrounge', 'to seek out one's fortune' – or, according to one early-seventeenth-century dictionary, 'to catch by hook or by crook'. Likewise, sixteenth-century Spanish had a similar word, *buscón*, which was used to mean 'swindler' or 'scoundrel'. Add these somewhat shady definitions into the mix alongside our toing-and-froing ship, and there's a strong argument to suggest that *busking* wasn't always as wholesome as it is today, and that the crew of our zigzagging ship might in fact have been pirates.

Whether or not *busking* was indeed once synonymous with piracy is debatable. This meaning had certainly emerged by the mid nineteenth century, when *busking* was defined in an 1867 *Sailor's Word-Book* as 'piratical cruising', but there's no actual written evidence before then. That might suggest that this piratical sense of the word was a later development, but this argument means ignoring all that earlier evidence from French and Spanish. Whatever the truth might be, it was the toing-and-froing of our *busking* ship that eventually led to the word *busk* being used more generally in English to mean 'to search or travel from place to place' – and if what you're searching for is an audience, or if you're funding your travels by giving public performances, then you're *busking* in the modern sense of the word. This meaning first appeared in the late eighteenth century and, while all others have steadily fallen out of use, has remained in place ever since.

ℬutler

was originally a servant in charge of a wine cellar

When you make someone the *butt* of the joke, you're using an Old French word for a target used in archery practice. When you *butt* into a conversation, you're using another Old French word, *boter*, meaning 'to shove'. Both your *butt* and your *buttocks* take their name (somewhat disparagingly) from an old Germanic word for the thick end of something. And when you drink wine or ale that has been stored in a *butt*, you're using the Latin word for a barrel or cask, *butis* – which is also, in a somewhat roundabout way, where the word *butler* originated.

The Latin *butis* had a diminutive form, *buticula*, which meant 'bottle'. This in turn led to an Old French word, *bouteillier*, which referred to a 'bottle-bearer' or 'cup-bearer', namely a servant in a royal court or noble household given the responsibility of serving the wine at meals and banquets.

Bouteillier was then imported into English after the Norman Conquest, and first began to appear in English texts in the late 1200s as *boteler* or *butuler*, and it's from here that the modern word *butler* eventually came about.

But all these medieval *botelers* and *butulers* weren't the stoic, smartly dressed heads of households that we might recognise today, and in fact their job was much closer to the French *bouteillier* than it was to the modern butler.

When it first appeared in the language in the thirteenth century, the word *butler* originally referred to a servant (or, in the royal household at least, to a personally appointed, high-ranking officer of the king or queen's court) specifically responsible for the upkeep and stocking of the wine-cellar, while all the other household duties now associated with butlering – such as serving food and setting out clothes for the day – would have been taken care of by other stewards and staff. So how did the role of the butler, and ultimately the meaning of the word *butler* itself, come to change?

Well, wine is an understandably expensive commodity. Not only that, but it is easy to steal, easy to replace with inferior liquor or to top up with water, and easy to lose or spoil if the casks it is kept in are allowed to fall into disrepair. Consequently, looking after the wine store of a royal or aristocratic household would once have been an extremely important task given only to the most trusted or responsible of servants, and it was this authority that led to the role of the butler steadily evolving over the years. By the nineteenth century, butlers were no longer merely wine-keepers but the heads of an entire hierarchy of servants and employees, responsible for everything from paying the household bills to tending the fires. But the original, literal meaning of the Victorian butler's job title was apparently never far away:

> The office of butler is thus one of very great trust in a household. Here, as elsewhere, honesty is the best policy: the butler should make it his business to understand the proper treatment of the different wines under his charge, which he can easily do from the wine-merchant, and faithfully attend to it; his own reputation will soon compensate for the absence of bribes from unprincipled wine-merchants . . . Nothing spreads more rapidly in society than the reputation of a good wine-cellar, and all that is required is wines well chosen and well cared for; and this a little knowledge, carefully applied, will soon supply.
>
> — Isabella Beeton, *Mrs Beeton's Book of Household Management* (1861)

Buxom

originally meant 'obedient'

On New Year's Day 1867, Connop Thirlwall, the Anglican bishop of St David's in south Wales, wrote a letter to a friend:

> Now do listen to my paternal admonitions; correct this fault, be a little more humble and modest, think better of your friends, and submit to their judgement . . . You will certainly be rewarded for this improvement in your conduct by a notable increase of tranquillity and cheerfulness in your view both of the past and of the future; and in the hope that you will be buxom and good, I conclude my New Year's lecture.

Needless to say that despite ending his letter in the hope that his friend will be 'buxom and good', Bishop Thirlwall wasn't making any kind of comment on their physical appearance. Instead, he was using a meaning of the word *buxom* that has long since disappeared from the language – and was, admittedly, already somewhat old-fashioned even by his day.

Buxom is a derivative of *búgan*, an Old English word variously used to mean 'to bend', 'to bow', 'to incline' or 'to submit'. The final *–om* is all that remains of the same suffix found in words like *handsome, tiresome, loathsome* and *quarrelsome*, which was used in Old English to form adjectives based on pre-existing words. Put those two together, and you'll arrive at something approaching the word's original meaning, and the meaning Bishop Thirlwall was employing in his letter: *buxom*, when it first began to appear in English texts way back in the twelfth century, meant simply 'obedient'.

By the Middle Ages, that meaning had developed slightly, so that *buxom* was now being used to mean 'compliant', 'obliging' and 'humble', and ultimately 'good-humoured', 'jolly', 'bright' and 'blithe' (which explains why Shakespeare somewhat puzzlingly describes the thieving soldier Bardolph as 'buxom' in *Henry V*). But to be good-humoured and jolly, it helps to be in good health – and it is because of that, that the meaning of the word *really* began to change.

In the late 1500s, *buxom* began to be used to describe people who appeared fit and healthy. At that time, being slightly plump or rotund was a sure sign of both a good diet and a strong constitution, and ultimately *buxomness* soon came to be associated with stoutness and shapeliness. In this sense, the word was originally applied to both sexes, and remained largely gender-neutral right up to the late nineteenth century: five years after he described a 'buxom dame about thirty' in *Peveril of the Peak* (1823), Sir Walter Scott described 'a buxom priest that thinks more of good living than of good life' in *The Fair Maid of Perth* (1828). But by the early 1900s, not only had this sense of 'stoutness' and hence 'shapeliness' eclipsed all other meanings of the word, but *buxom* had become associated almost exclusively with voluptuous women, and it is only in this sense that the word survives today.

Cheap

originally meant 'marketplace'

Typically describing anything low-cost, low-price or low-quality, nowadays the word *cheap* is used as an adjective. But long before all those meanings began to appear in the mid sixteenth century, *cheap* was both a noun and a verb, and was used in a number of contexts and with a number of meanings that have long since disappeared from the language.

At its very earliest, the word *cheap* derives from a Latin word, *caupo*, meaning 'pedlar' or 'tradesman' (as does the *chap* at the beginning of *Chapman*, incidentally). This then became the Old English word *céap*, which could be variously used as a noun, to mean 'trade', 'bargaining' or 'merchandise' (and in that latter sense was often used specifically of cattle), and as a verb to mean 'to purchase', 'to barter' or 'to strike a deal'.

Building on all of these early meanings, by the early Middle Ages *cheap* as a noun was being used more broadly to mean 'price', 'market' and even 'marketplace' (which is the meaning still found in place names like *Cheapside* and *Chipping Norton*). As a verb, its use had widened to mean 'to set a price', 'to make an offer' and 'to place a bid for something'. All in all, an array of different senses and meanings of *cheap* emerged during the word's early use in the language, with one glaring omission — not one of them referred to what we might now call a 'cheap' price.

Oddly, *cheap* started out as an entirely neutral term, used to refer to *any* sale or trade made at *any* price, good or bad. An inexpensive price or a fair deal ultimately had to be designated a 'good cheap', while a costlier product, a tougher market, or a harsher deal would be said to be a 'dear cheap' or an 'expensive cheap'. This remained the case right up to the sixteenth century, when *cheap* finally began to be used as an adjective in its own right and — presumably because everyone loves a bargain — came to refer only to inexpensive items and fair deals. Soon this more specialised meaning replaced the older, vaguer use of *cheap* altogether, leaving us with the word as we use it today. But what happened to the verb?

Well, around the same time that the adjective *cheap* first began to emerge in the 1500s, *cheapen* came along to replace the older use of *cheap* as a verb — although it too was originally a somewhat neutral term. On its debut appearance in the language, *cheapen* merely meant 'to ask the price of something', or 'to make an offer', but once the association between *cheapness* and good or low prices was fixed, *cheapen* too came to mean 'to haggle down a price', 'to make something cheap' — and hence, figuratively, 'to degrade' or 'to lower in estimation'. And it's these meanings that have remained in place ever since.

Cloud

originally meant 'rock'

Granted there aren't all that many overlaps between etymology and meteorology, but the fact remains that *cloud* comes from an Old English word, *clúd*, which once meant 'rock', 'hill' or 'mass of stone'. Because of that, *cloud* has some fairly unexpected etymological cousins in modern English, including *clod* and *clot*, as well as a handful of more obscure words like *clout* (a small piece of leather or iron, sheared from something larger), *cleat* (a wedge or bolt) and *clew* (a spherical globule or conglomeration of something smaller, such as a snowball or a ball of string — but more on that next . . .).

So how does a word for a mass of stone come to be used as a word for a mass of water vapour? Well, it's presumed that Old English speakers were quick to notice that thick, heavy, dark-grey rainclouds (the type that anyone living in England knows an awful lot about) looked – well, a lot like thick, heavy, dark-grey masses of rock. Consequently, the Old English word *clúd* soon gained a second meteorological meaning, and by the early fourteenth century this meaning had all but replaced the older one entirely; from the Middle English period onwards *clúd*, or *clod* as it had become by then, was being used almost exclusively to refer to clouds and it's this meaning that has endured ever since.

One question remains, though: if *clúd* meant 'rock', what was the Old English word for 'cloud'? The answer to that is *weolcen*, which is the origin of the somewhat old-fashioned English word *welkin*, meaning 'sky'. Sadly, *welkin* has all but disappeared from the language today outside of literary contexts and a handful of local dialects, but it remained in use right up to the late nineteenth century: you'll find it in Wordsworth, Longfellow, Sir Walter Scott and Charlotte Brontë among others, as well as in the original opening line of the Christmas favourite *Hark! The Herald Angels Sing*, once a solemn and considerably un-Christmassy hymn beginning 'Hark! how all the welkin rings'.

Just like *clúd*, however, *welkin* also changed its meaning over time. Although it originally meant 'cloud', its use steadily broadened and grew ever more figurative so that by the time Wordsworth, Longfellow, Brontë and the rest were using it in the nineteenth century, it was typically taken to mean 'the heavens', 'the firmament', 'the upper atmosphere' or 'the entirety of the sky'. Likewise, *to make the welkin ring,* or *to rend the welkin,* is an old-fashioned English expression describing an impossibly loud noise. Like a rock concert.

Clue

originally meant 'ball of string'

Remember that word *clew,* meaning 'a conglomeration of something smaller'? That's also the origin of the word *clue,* which long before it came to mean 'a piece of evidence' or 'a hint' originally meant a ball of string. But even more bizarrely than that, the story of how this change came about begins with a Greek myth involving a woman being impregnated by a bull. Hey, this is a Greek myth, after all.

The Cretan Bull was a gift by the Greek sea god Poseidon to King Minos of Crete, and was such an exceptionally fine animal that Minos refused to have it sacrificed and instead kept it for himself. Poseidon was understandably furious, and took revenge on Minos by having the goddess Aphrodite bewitch his wife, Pasiphaë, so that she would fall madly in love with it. Sure enough, nine months later she gave birth to a monstrous man-bull hybrid – the Minotaur.

Minos hid the Minotaur at the centre of the labyrinth and, to appease Poseidon, made an arrangement for a sacrifice of seven Athenian men and women to be sent into the maze every seven years for the creature to feast on. This practice continued for decades, until finally enough was enough – the heroic prince of Athens, Theseus, resolved to enter the labyrinth, kill the Minotaur, and end King Minos's gruesome sacrifices once and for all.

Taking the place of one of the latest batch of ill-fated tributes, Theseus travelled to Crete and immediately caught the eye of King Minos's young daughter, Ariadne. She agreed to help him in any way she could, and under cover of darkness led him to the entrance of the maze and armed him with a sword and a ball of string. All Theseus need do, Ariadne explained, was to tie one end of the string to the doorway of the maze and unravel the rest as he went. That way, no matter how deep into the maze he explored, he would always be able to find his way back out. Ariadne's plan worked perfectly, and after Theseus had found and killed the Minotaur, he simply retraced his steps and exited the labyrinth unscathed.

The story of Theseus and the Minotaur is one of the

most famous of all the Greek myths, and has been told and retold innumerable times over the centuries. Take this version by Geoffrey Chaucer, dating way back to 1385:

> Thereto have I a remedye in my thought,
> That, by a clewe of twyn, as he hath gon,
> The same were he may returne anon,
> Folwynge alwey the thred as he hath come.

Cut through all the jumbled Middle English and, yes, that 'clew of twine' is our ball of string – as well as the origin of what we would now call a *clue*.

Because Ariadne's *clew* helped guide Theseus through an otherwise bewildering, perplexing situation, as time went by the word came to be used more generally to mean 'something that points the way' or 'something useful that leads to a discovery'. By the seventeenth century, this meaning of *clew* (now spelled *clue*, thanks to the influence of French) had all but replaced the earlier one, and has survived to this day.

But what of Theseus, Ariadne and King Minos? Did they all live happily ever after? Well, Theseus went on to abandon Ariadne on the island of Naxos partway home, and when he arrived back in Athens, his father, King Aegeus, interpreted his ship's black sails as a sign that his son had been killed, and promptly threw himself into the Aegean Sea. King Minos meanwhile went on a deranged quest to track down

Daedalus, the architect of the labyrinth, but was killed on Sicily by being boiled alive in a bathtub. Not quite a happy ending then, but like I say – this is a Greek myth, after all.

Clumsy

originally meant 'numb with cold'

You know how it is. It's the depths of winter and you've just reached your front door. All you want is a hot cup of tea (or something stronger) and to come in out of the cold. Shivering, you reach into your coat pocket to grab your keys – only to find that your hands are so blisteringly cold that you can barely bend your fingers, never mind work your key into a tiny iced-up lock. So finally, with a frustrated groan, it slips from your grasp and vanishes into the heap of snow at your feet. Happy Christmas, indeed . . .

A few hundred years ago, if your hands were benumbed with cold like this, they were said to be *clumse*. The same word was also used in a number of figurative senses, including 'dull' or 'stupid', 'unresponsive' or 'slow-witted', 'idle' or 'unprepared', and even 'awkward', 'surly' or 'gruff', while one eighteenth-century *Universal Etymological English Dictionary* (1727) even lists *clumse* as a noun, meaning 'a numbskull' or 'one void of common sense'.

But long before then, in the early Middle Ages, *clumse* was used as a verb meaning 'to become stiff or numb with cold'. In this sense, it has been unearthed in texts dating back as far as the fourteenth century, but its origins probably lie even further back than that: similar words in languages such as Norwegian (*klump*, 'a lump'), Dutch (*kleumen*, 'to be blue with cold') and Icelandic (*klumsa*, 'speechless', 'dumbfounded', 'suffering from lockjaw') suggest that *clumse* might have some ancient Scandinavian or Germanic ancestor. But whatever that ancestor might have been, it is its descendants that we are more interested in here.

Around the same time that the adjective *clumse*-with-an-E began to appear in the language in the early 1600s, *clumsy*-with-a-Y also emerged. It too was originally used to mean 'numbed with cold' or 'frozen into inactivity' – just like your fingers, vainly searching for your keys – but over time this meaning began to shift, so that *clumsy* was soon being used to describe people or movements that are so awkward or ungainly that they gave the appearance of being 'numbed with cold'. So drop your key at your front door in the depths of winter, and you would be *clumse*. Drop your key at your front door at the height of the summer, and you would be *clumsy*.

From there, *clumsy* began to be used in all the figurative

senses we still use it in today: 'unskilful', 'poorly constructed', 'inelegant', 'difficult to use'. *Clumse* meanwhile largely fell out of use, although it and its derivatives still survive in a handful of local dialects: according to the *English Dialect Dictionary* (1898), *clumps* is an old Lincolnshire word meaning 'morose' or 'taciturn'; 'a clumpst fellow' is a 'plain-speaking fellow' in West Yorkshire; and the *Scottish National Dictionary* (1931) defines *clumpse* as 'to be hardly able to open mouth or speak by reason of thirst'. Where's that cup of tea when you need it?

Cubicle

originally meant 'bedroom'

There was a verb in Latin, *cubare*, that meant simply 'to lie down' or 'go to sleep'. From there, the English language has ended up with a whole host of words referring to some sense of reclining or going to bed. So if you're *recumbent* or *incumbent*, you're lying down. If you're *procumbent*, you're lying face down. A *concubine* is literally someone who lies with someone else. If you *secubate*, then you go to sleep alone. *Succumb* to something, and you yield to it (by literally lying down). To *accumb* means 'to lie down while eating a meal at a dinner table'. A bird *incubates* its eggs by sitting or roosting on top of them in its nest. An *incubus* is a hideous monster supposed to cause nightmares by sitting on someone while they're asleep. A *succubus* is a hideous monster supposed to cause nightmares by having sex with someone while they're asleep. And all of that – well, perhaps not all of it – might take place in your *cubicle*.

Cubicle comes from the Latin word *cubiculum*, meaning 'bedchamber', and it was as another word for a bedroom that it first appeared in the language in the late fifteenth century. After a century of use, however, *cubicle* suddenly disappeared: the *Oxford English Dictionary* has found no trace of it in print between 1513 and 1858, when it suddenly reappeared in reference to the bedrooms and dormitories in English boarding schools. From there, *cubicle* finally came to be applied to any small, secluded, partitioned space, set apart from whatever is around it and used for much more besides sleeping (depending on how interesting your job is, of course).

One question remains, though – why did *cubicle* disappear only to reappear centuries later? Admittedly, no one is quite sure, although not long before *cubicle* reappeared in the mid 1800s, the Latin word *cubiculum* was also lifted from obscurity and began to be used by archaeologists and architects to refer to crypts, catacombs and burial chambers. Perhaps one word being plucked from the history books merely led to the resurrection of another? It's a plausible idea. But best to sleep on it.

&Cupboard

originally meant 'table'

A *cup* is a cup, and a *board* is a board — so why is a *cupboard* a 'cup board'? After all, a *board* is a flat, wooden panel for putting things *on*, not a closed cabinet for putting things *in*. So how on earth did we get from A to B? (Or, as the case may be, from B to C?)

The answer is simply that a *cupboard* has not always been a cupboard. Back when the word first emerged in the late 1300s, a *cupboard* was actually a table: a literal 'cup-board' or flat table-top used for serving, storing or displaying cups and crockery. (Likewise a *sideboard* too was originally a table, only one kept literally at the 'side' of a room.)

No one is entirely sure why, but by the early sixteenth century that meaning had altered so that a *cupboard* was no long a table used to display crockery, but a closed cabinet or recess in which cups, plates, dishes and other vessels could be displayed or stored until required. By the seventeenth century, people were also using these newly defined *cupboards* to store food (*to cry cupboard* even meant 'to crave food' in the late 1600s), and by the mid nineteenth century, people were finally finding skeletons in their cupboards:

> Was it an Englishman or a Frenchman who first remarked that every family had a skeleton in its cupboard? I am not learned enough to know, but I reverence the observation, whoever made it. It speaks a startling truth through an appropriately grim metaphor – a truth which I have discovered by practical experience. Our family had a skeleton in the cupboard, and the name of it was Uncle George.
> – Wilkie Collins, *The Queen of Hearts* (1859)

But if you think the change from 'table' to 'cupboard' seems peculiar, the Italian word *credenza* has an even stranger history. Nowadays, a *credenza* is a low sideboard or free-standing cupboard, but the word's literal meaning is the same as the English word *credence* – namely 'belief', 'trust' or 'credibility'. The change in meaning here is down to little more than the paranoia of medieval royals and nobles, who were so terrified of being poisoned that they would demand someone else taste their food before they did. Consequently any food that was brought to them would be first placed on a *credenza*, where its literal 'trustworthiness' could be tested by some unlucky servant. If the servant survived, the food would be deemed safe, whereas if the servant died — well, at least he got a free meal out of it . . .

To Curry Favour

originally meant 'to groom a chestnut horse'

An old bit of language folklore will have you believe that *currying favour* with someone — that is, obsequiously ingratiating yourself with them for personal gain — is based around the image of gradually mixing yourself into their group until you're finally admitted into it, just as the flavours in a curry slowly work their way throughout the dish. It's another nice theory certainly, but again it's completely untrue.

That kind of *curry* takes its name from a Tamil word for a sauce or relish, *karil,* that first appeared in English in the late sixteenth century in the journals of a Dutch merchant sailor named Jan Huygen van Linschoten:

Most of their *[the people of India's]* fish is eaten with rice, which they seeth in broth, which they put upon the rice, and is somewhat sour, as if it were sodden in gooseberries or unripe grapes, but it tasteth well.

– Jan Huygen van Linschoten, *A Discourse of Voyages into the East and West Indies* (1598)

The *curry* of *currying favour* is an old French word, *corrier*, which literally means 'to groom a horse'. This sense of the word has largely fallen out of use in English – although horse groomers are still sometimes known as *curriers*, while the tanning or treatment of leather or animal hide is also somewhat archaically known as *currying*. But if that's the *curry*, what's the *favour*? Well, take a look at this sixteenth-century proverb:

He thatt wylle in courte abyde, must cory favelle bake and syde, for souche gett moste gayne.

– Thomas Underhill, *Narratives of the Days of the Reformation* (*c.* 1561)

In other words, 'everyone in the royal court must curry favour at every opportunity in order to make the greatest possible personal gain'. Tellingly, the word *favour* here has been replaced by 'favelle' – an old fourteenth-century word for a chestnut-coloured horse, which is in turn derived from its earlier French equivalent, *fauve*, or *favvel*. So what does grooming a chestnut-coloured horse have to do with acting obsequiously?

The missing link here is a medieval French narrative poem called the *Roman de Fauvel*, or 'Story of Fauvel'. The eponymous Fauvel was a chestnut-coloured horse, whose name was an abbreviation of the six vices *flaterie* (flattery), *avarice, vilanie* (vileness), *varieté* (variability), *envie* (envy) and *lascheté* (laxity). In the story, Fauvel decides to try to take over his master's house, and with the help of 'Dame Fortune' (a personification of fate) uses every trick in the book to rise to considerable prominence in the French royal household and soon has all the leaders of the church and state fawning over him. Before long, everyone is quite literally 'currying Fauvel'.

Fauvel's tale proved immensely popular in its day, and soon 'currying a chestnut-coloured horse' had become a well-known metaphor for ingratiating yourself with someone to improve your own standing. Having first appeared in English in the early 1400s, the phrase had morphed into 'currying favour' by the turn of the century and has remained in use ever since.

Deer

originally meant 'animal'

In 970 AD, Aldred, the provost of Chester-le-Street in County Durham, took it upon himself to go through his Latin copy of the gospels and add his own handwritten notes and translations beneath each line. It just so happens that the gospels held at Chester-le-Street Minster at that time weren't just any old copy, but the Lindisfarne Gospels, an immaculately illustrated and illuminated text that was already nearly three centuries old by the time Aldred unthinkingly added his contribution.

That's not to say that Aldred's annotations did anything to spoil the priceless manuscript on which he was writing them. Far from it in fact, as his line-by-line notes now comprise the oldest surviving translation of the Gospels in the history of our language, and are one of the most cherished texts held by the British Library. But how does Aldred's defacing – sorry, translating – of a priceless religious document concern us here?

It all comes down to the famous final verse of chapter 28 of the Gospel of St Luke: 'For it is easier for a camel to go through a needle's eye, than for a rich man to enter into the kingdom of God.' Beneath the Latin word *camelum*, Aldred wrote '*se camal þæt micla dear*', or 'the camel, that great deer'. Admittedly, tenth-century Northumbrian clergymen probably weren't all that knowledgeable when it came to desert-dwelling mammals, but Aldred seemingly confusing a camel for a deer wasn't a sign of his lack of knowledge, nor of a linguistic oversight. In fact, given the period in which he was writing, it was a perfectly accurate description.

The Old English word for 'deer' was *déor* – but that was also the Old English word for a camel. And a lion, for that matter. And a wolf. A wild boar could be a *déor*. So could a bear, a fox and a badger. In fact, the word *déor* could apply to any number of creatures, as it was originally simply another word for any large, undomesticated mammal. In that sense, our word *deer* began life as an equivalent of what we would now call a *beast*, and indeed it was the adoption of the French word *beste* in the thirteenth century that likely compelled the meaning of *déor* to change: with *beast* now added to our vocabulary, there was little need for English speakers to retain an older byword for a large mammal, and so *déor* steadily specified, eventually attaching itself to deer (probably in part due to their size, and in part due to their use as a food source). By the turn of the fifteenth century this was the only surviving meaning of *deer* in use in English, while the older, more generalised use has long since disappeared.

Defecation

originally meant 'purification'

Remember a few pages back when we were talking about *bum-fodder* and *arsewisps*? Well, hold your nose, because we're heading down that way again. Let's get to the bottom (no pun intended) of *defecation*.

Unsurprisingly, at the centre of the word *defecate* is *faeces*, which is the plural form of a singular word, *faex*, borrowed into English from Latin in the late fifteenth century. Oddly, *faeces* has been used to mean 'excrement' only since the early 1600s (you were warned about this . . .) while its original meaning, in both English and Latin, was merely 'dregs' or 'waste'. In particular, it referred to the yeasty, sedimentary waste material or 'lees' found at the bottom of wine casks after fermentation, but besides that *faeces* could also be used in Latin to refer to face paint or make-up and to the brine used to pickle vegetables. Cicero even referred to the lowest of the lower classes as the *faex populi*, or the 'dregs' of society, while the Roman poet Martial called his last few remaining pennies his *faece locelli*, or 'the dregs of his moneybox'. Clearly, *faeces* was a much more useful and varied word to the Romans than it has since become for us. It certainly shouldn't be pooh-poohed. (OK, so maybe *that* pun was intended.)

So if that's *faeces* taken care of, what about *defecate?* Well, the *de–* of *defecate* is a Latin prefix used to express removal, reversal or an undoing of something. So while the Latin verb *decorare* meant 'to bestow an honour' or 'to adorn' (and is the origin of the English word *decorate*), the verb *dedecorare* meant 'to dishonour' or 'to strip away' (and is the origin of the seldom-used word *dedecorate*, meaning 'to bring shame on' or 'to disgrace'). Likewise the Latin verb *defaecare* meant 'to cleanse of dregs', 'to wash away sediment' or 'to rid of impurities', and it was this meaning that was carried through into English when *defecate* made its first appearance in the language in the late sixteenth century:

> A-mornings, I rise ordinarily at seven o'clock . . .
> I drink me up a good bowl of ale: when in a
> sweet-pot it is defecated by all night's standing, the
> drink is the better . . . a morsel in a morning with
> a sound draught is very wholesome and good for the
> eyesight.
>
> – Robert Langham,
> a letter (1575)

You'd be forgiven for thinking that something that had been defecated 'in a sweet-pot' and then left to stand all night wouldn't be the most 'wholesome' thing to consume first thing in the morning. But when you know that *defecation* originally meant simply 'purification' or 'clarification', suddenly Langham's early-morning eye-opener – quite literally – becomes clear . . .

𝔇ismantle

originally meant 'to remove a cloak'

Etymology often throws together bunches of seemingly disparate words that, with a little bit of historical context, end up being long-lost cousins of one another. Take, for instance, the verb *dismantle*, meaning 'to take apart'. Its relatives include the *mantelpiece* above your fireplace, the enormous *manta* rays of the tropical oceans, and *portmanteau* words, those formed by smushing two existing words together to form a new one (like *smush*, from *smash* and *mush*). As that recurrent 'mant' suggests, all four of these words are related, but precisely what it is that connects them has long since vanished from their meanings. So to find out what's going on, we need to dismantle *dismantle*.

The word *dismantle* literally means 'to remove a mantle' – a type of long, loose, sleeveless cloak popular in the Middle Ages:

. . . take your sweetheart's hat,
And pluck it o'er your brows, muffle your face,
Dismantle you, and, as you can, disliken
The truth of your own seeming, that you may . . .
Get undescribed.
            — William Shakespeare, *A Winter's Tale* (*c.* 1600)

In other words, cover your face and take your coat off, and hopefully no one will know it's you. In this sense, *dismantle* comes from the Latin word for 'cloak,' *mantellum*, which is also the missing piece of the puzzle connecting all the other words we mentioned above.

Mantelpieces were originally called 'manteltrees', and earned their name because the heavy beam or shelf they comprise covers a fire much like a cloak or mantle enshrouds its wearer. *Manta* rays were so called by the Spanish sailors who first saw them and reckoned they resembled immense cloaks floating in the water:

The name 'manta' has not been improperly given to this fish . . . for it being broad and long like a quilt, it wraps its fins around a man or any other animal that happens to come within its reach, and immediately squeezes it to death.

                                — Antonio de Ulloa,
                    A Voyage to South America (trans. 1758)

(Not quite – they're actually harmless plankton eaters.) And *portmanteau* words take their name from that of a French dual-compartment suitcase, in which you can literally 'carry' (*porter*) your cloak (*manteau*). It was Lewis Carroll who first called blended words 'portmanteaux' in *Through the Looking-glass* (1871): as Humpty Dumpty explains when Alice asks the meaning of *slithy*, words formed by amalgamating two existing words are, 'like a portmanteau – there are two meanings packed up into one word'.

oom

was originally a law

A king's work is never done, it seems – not even at Christmas. According to the *Anglo-Saxon Chronicle*, a record of English history kept from the ninth to twelfth centuries, in the year 1085:

> At midwinter the king *[William the Conqueror]* was at Gloucester . . . and had deep speech with his counsellors, and sent men all over England to each shire

> to find out what or how much each landholder had
> in land and livestock, and what it was worth.

Twenty years after conquering England, William I wanted to ensure that his imposition of Norman rule across England was bringing in the appropriate amount of revenue, and so commissioned an enormous survey of (almost) his entire kingdom to assess the precise value of every landowner's assets. The result, completed the following year, was his 'great inquisition or survey of the lands of England' – the Domesday Book.

William himself never actually knew his survey as the Domesday Book, as that nickname (which retains the Middle English spelling of *doom*) did not emerge until the late 1180s, almost a century after his death. So where did it come from?

Doom was originally a legal term in Old English essentially meaning 'judgement', 'law', 'justice' or 'statute'. Despite appearances, it is actually related to the verb *do* (in the sense of making or putting in place laws and other directives), as well as the *–dom* of words like *kingdom*, *wisdom*, *martyrdom* and *boredom*. Old English courtrooms were consequently *doom-halls*, while judges or *doomsmen* would pronounce sentences from their *doom-stools*. This legal use of *doom* survived right through to the nineteenth century (albeit becoming increasingly literary and archaic over time), but has long since fallen out of use today. In its place has emerged a much more ominous meaning of *doom*, carrying connotations of failure, death, destruction — and a very different kind of *doomsday*.

These relatively more recent meanings of *doom* derive from the notion of mankind being 'judged', just as Anglo-Saxon criminals were in their *doom-halls*. Hence the name Domesday Book is partly based on the legal sense of *doom* (in the sense that the king's survey was a final and unquestionable authority), and partly an allusion to the final, unquestionable judgements doled out on mankind on Judgement Day (or *doomsday*). In the words of Richard FitzNeal, treasurer in the court of William's great-grandson, Henry II:

> When this book is appealed to on those matters which it contains, its sentence cannot be quashed or set aside with impunity. That is why we have called it 'the Book of Judgement' . . . not because it contains decisions on various difficult points, but because its decisions, like those of the Last Judgement, are unalterable.
>
> — Richard FitzNeal,
> *Dialogues Concerning the Exchequer* (*c.* 1187)

Drench

*originally meant
'to ply someone with drink'*

There's something to be said for the sheer number of words relating to drink, drunks and drinking to excess that there are in the English language. Besides the likes of *inebriate* and *intoxicate*, our dictionaries are full of all kinds of inventive and unusual synonyms for drunkenness, from being *on the mop* (a reference to the carousing behaviour of those attending nineteenth-century employment fairs or 'mops') to *making a Virginia fence* (an allusion to walking in a zigzag, like a fence made of interlocking timbers). In the Middle Ages, you could be *cup-shotten*, *sack-sopped* and *tup-shackled*. The Tudors went *shoeing the goose* and *swallowing the tavern-token*. In the seventeenth century, people began *fuddling their caps* and *hunting tavern-foxes*. The Victorians *boiled* and *scammered* themselves until they were *hit under the wing* or ended up *down among the dead men* if they passed out among the empties on the floor of a pub. And in 1920s America, drinkers bypassed the Prohibition laws down at their local speakeasy by *going on a toot*, *getting ossified* and *drenching their gizzards*. But as it turns out, the association between *drench* and drinking runs a lot more deeply than that.

Linguistically speaking, *drench* began life as the causative form of the Old English verb *drencan* – in other words, while *drencan* was Old English for 'drink' (which made an inn a *drenc-hús*, and a drinking vessel a *drenc-cuppe*), the ancestors of *drench* were all words carrying some sense of causing a drinking to take place. So when it first appeared in the language more than a thousand years ago, *drench* variously meant 'to make to drink', 'to serve drink to' and even 'to forcibly administer a draught of medicine'. As a verb, *drench* is still sometimes used in veterinary contexts in the sense of administering a medicine, but by far its most familiar use is as a synonym of words such as *soak* and *saturate*. But where did that meaning come from?

Well, as well as meaning simply 'to drink', back in Old English the verb *drencan* could also be used to mean 'to submerge in liquid' (which made a *drenc-flód* a great storm or deluge, particularly one that had led to loss of life). That meant that, as the causative form of the verb, one of the earliest meanings of the word *drench* was 'to drown' or 'to sink'. It's from there that the use of *drench* to mean 'to wet' or 'to soak thoroughly' first appeared in the early thirteenth century, and while most other meanings of the word have since disappeared, this one has remained in place ever since.

Dump

originally meant 'daydream'

It's tempting to presume that when we describe someone as being *down in the dumps*, we're talking about the same 'dump' that we send our rubbish off to — after all, they're both fairly unpleasant places to be. In actual fact, however, the two are entirely unrelated.

The *dump* of 'rubbish dump' dates back only as far as the early 1800s, but is derived from the much older use of *dump* as a verb meaning 'to drop' or 'to cast off forcibly'. The verb *dump* dates back to the fourteenth century in English, and is thought to have been borrowed into the language from an even older Scandinavian source; at its very earliest, it was probably originally onomatopoeic, and might have been intended to echo the sound of something being thrown, dropped or discarded with a dull thud.

The *dump* of 'down in the dumps' — which is, incidentally, the earliest use of the noun *dump* recorded in English — dates back to the sixteenth century, and originally referred to a dazed, unfocused, preoccupied state of mind. Put another way, a *dump* was originally a daydream.

Frustratingly, no one is entirely sure from where this use of *dump* derives. One theory is that it is somehow related to the German word *dumpf*, meaning 'dull', 'flat' or 'hollow'. Another claims that it comes from an old Dutch word, *domp*, meaning 'mist' or 'haze', and which is a distant cousin of our word *damp*. Whatever its origins, being down in the dumps – or just *in a dump*, as was said originally – hasn't always been a bad thing.

When it first appeared in the language in the early sixteenth century, this kind of *dump* tended only to be used of dazed or slightly perplexed states of mind, or to the inattentive, preoccupied feelings caused by considering something so intently that your mind wanders away from everything else. One seventeenth-century *Dictionarie of the French and English Tongues* (1611) even gives 'to put into a dump' as a translation of an old French expression, *donner la muse à quelqu'un*, meaning 'to muse over something'. But by the mid 1500s, things had taken a turn for the worse. The melancholic, low-spirited version of the *dump* that we know today had begun to emerge, and by the late seventeenth century this much less optimistic meaning had replaced the earlier more neutral one. Today, in this sense at least, it remains the only meaning of the word still in use.

Eager

originally meant 'acrid'

In the interests of keeping scientific jargon to a minimum (we've already dealt with the sublimation of crystalline stibnite, after all), let's keep this brief: given enough time and oxygen, a culture of *Acetobacter* bacteria will transform a dilute solution of ethanol into weak acetic acid. In other words, it will change alcohol into vinegar. How that process occurs doesn't concern us here (basically, it's all down to oxidation). But the word *vinegar* does.

Vinegar has been known about since antiquity, and was probably first produced by accident – through spoiling wine during the fermentation process – in Ancient Egypt. To the Ancient Greeks, vinegar was called *oxos*, a name meaning 'sharp' or 'acidic' (and from which *oxygen* takes its name, as it was once thought to be common to all acids). To the Romans, vinegar was *acetum*, a name essentially meaning 'sourness' (and from which the *acetabulum*, the socket that the ball of the thigh bone sits inside, also takes its name – which literally means 'little vinegar saucer'). And to the Anglo-Saxons, vinegar was *ecced*, an Old English corruption of the Romans' *acetum*. That name would have remained in use in England were it not for the Norman Conquest, which ousted *ecced* from the vocabulary and replaced it with its Old French equivalent, *vyn egre*, or literally 'eager wine'. It's from here that the word *vinegar* eventually emerged — and it's also from here that we can pick up the story of *eager*.

Calling vinegar 'eager wine' doesn't mean that it's ready and willing to do whatever necessary, of course, no matter how good it might taste with chips. In this sense, *eager* means 'pungent' or 'acrid', and like *ecced* and *acetum* before it (as well as *acerbic* and *exacerbate*) is descended from a Latin word, *acer*, meaning 'acrid' or 'sharp'. But as time went by, *eager* came to be used to refer to much more than just sharp, acidic flavours. Shakespeare used it to refer to harsh, icy coldness. Chaucer used it both to refer to particularly potent, effective medicine, and to sharp, biting words. On its earliest appearance in English in the late thirteenth century, it meant 'fierce' or 'angry'. A century after that, it was being used to describe wild animals. A century after that, it was being used by falconers to describe hungry birds of prey, and it's perhaps in allusion to the apparently insatiable appetite of wild beasts and birds that *eager* finally began to be used to describe someone with an intense, impatient desire for something by the mid 1500s — the meaning that has remained in use ever since.

Explode

originally meant 'to jeer a performer off a stage'

In eighteenth-century slang, *trunk-makers* were theatrical patrons who, rather than cheer or applaud, pounded their fists on the seats and railings to show their appreciation. The racket they made would echo down noisily throughout the auditorium – and apparently sounded like a trunk-maker hammering together a wooden trunk. With that in mind, take a look at this quote from Henry Fielding's *Tom Jones*:

> This somewhat may be indeed resembled to the famous trunk-maker in the playhouse; for, whenever the person who is possessed of it doth what is right, no ravished or friendly spectator is so eager or so loud in his applause: on the contrary, when he doth wrong, no critic is so apt to hiss and explode him.
>
> – Henry Fielding,
> *The History of Tom Jones, a Foundling* (1749)

Besides *trunk-maker*, there's another word in that extract that probably requires a little extra explanation – because a theatrical critic threatening to 'explode' an actor from the stage certainly isn't thinking of doing so with some kind of makeshift explosive device. *Explode* is actually a derivative of the Latin verb *plaudere*, meaning 'to clap the hands', which makes it a somewhat unexpected etymological cousin of words such as *applause, plausible* and *plaudit*. Added to that is the prefix *ex–*, used to form words with some sense of an outward movement or removal, like *exclude, exhale* and *excursion*. Put those two elements together and you have a word meaning 'to deride', 'to reject scornfully' or 'to jeer a performer from a stage', which was the original meaning of *explode*, and the meaning used by Henry Fielding in the extract above. But how did we get from there, to – well, an *explosion*?

In the mid 1600s, around a century after it first appeared in the language, *explode* began to broaden. Alongside still being used to mean 'to jeer' or 'to mock', it began to be used more loosely to mean 'to emit' or 'to give off', and by extension, 'to drive or push out suddenly, noisily or violently'. Eventually, by the late eighteenth century, *explode* was being used to refer to the noisy, violent 'explosions' caused by gases, gunpowder, bombs and other combustible materials, and it's from there that our most familiar meaning of the word eventually developed.

One question remains though: if that's how *explode* and *applause* are connected, where do *plaudit* and *plausible* come into it?

Well, if something is *plausible* then it is literally 'worthy of applause' (while the opposite is true if something is *implausible*). *Plaudit*, however, is more complicated: it began life as *plaudite!*, the imperative form of the verb *plaudere* literally used as a command to applaud. Back in Ancient Rome, *plaudite!* would have been shouted by the performers at the end of a play to request applause from the audience – who would either comply or refuse, depending on the success of the play – and it's through association with a performer being 'honoured' with applause that the word *plaudit* eventually came to mean a prize or accolade.

Exquisite

originally meant 'searched for'

When we describe something as *exquisite*, we tend to mean that it is truly, stunningly beautiful. We might talk of an *exquisite* meal, an *exquisite* painting, or an *exquisite* piece of music. But what about an *exquisite* pain? An *exquisite* disease? Or *exquisite* torture? To modern ears, these might seem strange, old-fashioned or just plain wrong. But at one time, they would have made perfect sense.

Exquisite literally means 'sought out': at its centre is the Latin verb *quaerere*, meaning 'to seek' or 'search', to which is added the same *ex–* of *explode*, meaning 'out' or 'outward'. Consequently, when it first appeared in the language in the mid fifteenth century, *exquisite* was used to describe anything that had been searched or striven for, carefully or specifically chosen, or else attained only after great effort or ingenuity. But that was only the beginning.

If you're searching or striving for something, then you can presume that it's fairly difficult to find, and that implication soon led to *exquisite* being used to describe anything rare or exceptional, or obscure and far-fetched (hence Shakespeare refers to an 'exquisite reason' in *Twelfth Night*). But to uncover something rare or obscure, you'll first have to be dedicated and precise in your search, which was the next meaning *exquisite* took under its wing. By the mid sixteenth century, it was being used to describe anything highly wrought, or the product of keen, concerted, exacting work – so an *exquisite* knowledge would be one that is highly informed, while an *exquisite* study or investigation would be noticeably thorough and accurate.

By the late 1500s that meaning had changed again, and *exquisite* next came to be used to describe anything that was the product of this kind of dedicated, exacting knowledge or work – but that 'product' could be both good and very, very bad. *Exquisite* torture was elaborately thought-through torture, designed to be as exactingly painful as possible. An *exquisite* pain was a particularly intense one. An *exquisite* disease was one that had either been perfectly accurately diagnosed, or else was an unerringly accurate textbook case.

Finally, around the turn of the sixteenth century, *exquisite* began to be used of anything that was not only the product of keenly informed and dedicated work, but was the pinnacle or quintessence of its type — in other words, an example of pure excellence. As all the older meanings of the word fell out of use, this final meaning soon established itself as the word's foremost, and has remained in use through to today.

Fathom

originally meant 'to embrace'

As a noun, the word *fathom* refers to a length or depth of precisely six feet. As a verb, it means 'to comprehend' or 'to understand'. But despite these apparently dissimilar definitions, both these senses of the word are actually related.

The Old English ancestor of *fathom* was *fæðm*, but unlike either of the meanings above it was used to mean 'a person's outstretched arms'. This definition survived for a time in English in the old expression *to make a fathom*, meaning 'to stretch your arms out as wide as possible', but has long since fallen out of use. Both the meanings that have survived, however, can trace their origins back to here.

The size of a man's outstretched arms, from fingertip to fingertip, originally formed the basis of the measurement we now call a *fathom*. Today, that measurement is standardised to precisely six feet, but back in Old English things weren't quite so fixed and there was a considerable amount of flexibility (not least because arms tend to come in all sorts of shapes and sizes). One of the earliest written records of a *fathom*, for instance, comes from a ninth-century glossary of Latin and English that equates it to a Roman measurement known as a *passus*. That would put it closer to five feet rather than six, as a *passus* was based on the size of a Roman soldier's pace, from one foot leaving the ground behind the body to it touching the ground again in front. Another definition, taken from a separate Latin glossary compiled two centuries later, equates a *fathom* with a *cubit*, a measurement of roughly 18 inches based on the length of a man's forearm. Confusingly, both these definitions seemingly co-existed for a time, before the fingertip-to-fingertip explanation finally established itself as the standard in the early Middle Ages.

So what about the verb *fathom*? That too can be traced back to that Anglo-Saxon man with his arms outstretched.

By the early fourteenth century, *fathom* was being used to mean 'to hug' or 'to embrace with the arms', while if two people *fathomed together*, then they cuddled one another. But as the use of a *fathom* as a measurement became more established, the verb *fathom* followed suit: soon it came to be used to mean 'to measure the size of something', either using your outstretched arms as a guide, or else a 'fathom line', a six-foot weighted plumb-line used to measure depth. From there, it didn't take long for more figurative uses of the verb to emerge, and by the mid seventeenth century *fathom* had come to mean 'to get to the bottom of something', and ultimately, 'to thoroughly understand'.

Fetish

originally meant 'talisman'

In 1689, a young British chaplain named John Ovington was hired by the East India Company to travel to Asia to minister to the company's Indian workers. After two years' work he returned to Europe and published an account of his journey, *A Voyage to Surat*, in 1696. In it he recalled coming across an African tribe near the delta of the River Congo on Africa's west coast — and finding out all about their 'fetishes':

They travel nowhere without their fetish about them, one of which looks like the small end of a stag's horn, with a bell tied to it, about the bigness of a man's thumb. But each of them had his own made of such materials as the priests . . . think fit to bestow upon them.

— John Ovington,
A Voyage to Surat in the Year 1689 (1696)

As fetishes go, carrying around a piece of horn with a bell on it everywhere you go might seem fairly tame, but needless to say these West African *fetishes* were not the ones we talk about today.

When it first appeared in the language in the early seventeenth century, the word *fetish* originally referred to African amulets or charms that, as Ovington goes on to explain, 'are supposed to act upon natural things, so as to drive away from any place, rain, hail, or wild and venomous beasts'. In this sense, *fetish* found its way into English via the Portuguese explorers and merchant sailors who travelled and traded their way down the African coast in the sixteenth century, and who used their word for a talisman or a magic spell, *feitiço*, to refer to the local tribes' talismans. (In turn, this Portuguese word is descended from the Latin *facticius*, literally meaning 'artificial' or 'man-made', implying that these charms and amulets were little more than material objects bestowed with magical or supernatural powers.)

Popularised by anthropologists and religious scholars in the eighteenth century, this talismanic meaning of *fetish* remained in place in English right through to the late 1800s. It was then that it was picked up and applied to the newly emerging science of psychoanalysis, which finally established the modern *fetish* as it is today.

Because these talismans and amulets were merely inanimate objects revered by their holders, in the late nineteenth century the term *fetishism* came to be used to refer to an erotic desire or obsession for a non-sexual object. Later discussed in detail by the likes of Sigmund Freud and Carl Jung, the earliest description of this kind of behaviour emerged in 1897, when the English physician Havelock Ellis wrote of a kind of 'sexual inversion' he had observed in which 'a woman's hair, or foot, or even clothing, becomes the focus of a man's sexual aspirations'. Helpfully, he provided evidence of a fine example:

> Casanova, an acute student and lover of women, who was in no degree a foot fetichist, remarks that all men who share his interest in women are attracted by their feet; they offer the same interest, he considers, as the question of the particular edition offers to the book-lover . . . It would seem that even animals have

a certain amount of sexual consciousness in the feet;
I have noticed a male donkey, just before coitus, bite
the feet of his partner.

– Havelock Ellis,
Studies in the Psychology of Sex, Vol. 5 (1906)

Fiasco

originally meant 'broken bottle'

Imagine you're at the theatre. The show gets off to an inaus-
picious start when the curtain fails to open properly, and
then, as the first performer takes to the stage, he trips up.
After stumbling through his opening speech, he's joined by
another actor who misses his cue. In the background, an
extra knocks over a prop and it smashes onto the stage. And
so the show goes on, disaster after disaster, until finally the
curtain falls and the performers are *exploded* from the stage.
In a word, it's a total fiasco.

In its native Italian, a *fiasco* is literally a glass bottle, and
in particular a bulb-shaped chianti bottle of the kind that is
usually partly wrapped in a decorative, cushioning covering of
straw. Sometime in the Middle Ages however, the word fell

into use in Italian slang among the actors and performers of the time, who began referring to making a mistake on stage as *far fiasco*, or 'to make a bottle'. A *fiasco* ultimately became a theatrical calamity – just like that mentioned above – that somehow led to the performance coming to a premature end, and these theatrical connotations were still in place when the word appeared in English for the first time, in a letter between two Victorian statesmen, Lord Lonsdale and John Wilson Croker, in 1855:

> My dear Croker, *[The Earl of]* Derby has made what the theatrical people call a fiasco. He would not make a Ministry from his own friends or his own bat ... I am told that the House of Commons is becoming more unmanageable every session.

But how did a word for a chianti bottle ever come to mean a calamity in the first place? Admittedly, no one is entirely sure – but there is no shortage of theories.

One explanation claims that the term might have been inspired by an incident like that described above, in which some hapless actor or extra dropped a bottle on stage, ruining a performance. Another claims that it refers to actors drowning their sorrows after a badly received show, perhaps only for their drink to be spilled or smashed just when things seemingly can't get any worse. A more plausible theory is that the phrase might have started out among glassblowers, before finding its way onto the stage: perhaps if an error were made in the creation of some ornate piece of glassware, the blower might smash the mistake and reuse the glass to make a bog-standard wine bottle.

Whatever the connection may be, it was the hapless and luckless performers of Renaissance Italy who first attached connotations of failure to the word *fiasco*. From there, it was borrowed first into French and then into English nearly two centuries ago, before quickly becoming more generalised. As a result, ever since the late nineteenth century we have been able to describe any embarrassing disaster or debacle – either on stage or off – as a total *fiasco*.

Finance

originally meant 'ransom'

Remember a few pages back, when we found out that banks were originally benches? And that a *bankrupt* tradesman would have his insolvency made public by having his bench destroyed – or rather, his 'bank ruptured'? Well, it turns out that *bankruptcy* isn't the only word from the world of finance to have a somewhat alarming history.

A *broker*, for instance, was originally a pedlar of shoddy, second-hand goods. A *mortgage* is literally a 'death pledge', a contract entered into that only comes to an end when the debt is repaid or the debtor perishes. And as for the word *finance* itself, it can trace its history back to the murky world of ransom and imprisonment.

Finance derives via French from *finer*, a Latin verb essentially meaning 'to end', or 'to settle a dispute'. This literal meaning was still intact when the word *finance* first appeared in English in the early fifteenth century as simply another word for an ending or termination, but the monetary sense of the word was not far behind.

Finer had a number of much more specific meanings in Latin, including 'to settle a debt', 'to pay or bargain for something' and even 'to ransom' – a meaning that soon began to surface in English too. The *Oxford English Dictionary* has uncovered an account of a £1,200 loan made to the Earl of Somerset 'for the payment of his fenaunce' (i.e. to secure his release from prison) dating from as far back as 1439. A few decades after that, the word *finance* began to be used as a verb meaning 'to put to ransom', the earliest record of which comes from an account dating from 1478 of a violent attack on the Archbishop of York and his entourage as they forded the River Swale, near Helperby in North Yorkshire:

On the said assault and pursuit were taken, yolden *[sur-rendered]*, and holden as prisoners by the said misdoers Peres of Cawood, and Thomas Mayne, squires, Henry Fox, yeoman, and *[some]* of the said Cardinal's servants; and some of them laboured and treated by them to make finance, as *[if]* they had been the King's enemies, and many and divers of them despoiled of their horses, harnesses and also gold and silver.

– Sir Edward Plumpton,
a letter (1478)

The attack on the archbishop and his retinue was carried out by the tenants of the surrounding area in protest over the payment of tolls for the use of the land. In the ambush, several of the archbishop's men were killed, while others were captured and taken 'to make finance' – or, in other words, held for ransom.

The use of *finance* to mean 'ransom' survived in English for another century, before disappearing in the late 1500s to be replaced by broader, less specific meanings: by the turn of the seventeenth century, *finance* was being used to mean 'taxation', 'the borrowing of money at interest' and 'the supply of goods and services'; by the eighteenth century, these meanings too had fallen out of use, and *finance* was finally being used to mean 'the management of money', or 'the monetary resources of a company or individual'; and the verb *finance*, meaning 'to provide capital for an enterprise', appeared in the mid nineteenth century. Today, these monetary associations are the only uses of the word *finance* to survive – while happily the word's darker past has drifted into history.

Flirt

originally meant 'sneer'

When the word *flirt* first fluttered into life in the language back in the late Middle Ages, it originally referred to a sudden, short twitching or jerking movement. It's thought that the word itself might even have been coined onomatopoeically – like *flick*, *flip* and *flit* – to represent precisely the same kind of flittering, flickering movement to which it referred. Back in the mid 1500s, *flirt* was being used to denote all kinds of hurried movements, from a hard rap or tap with the knuckles to a sharp flick with a finger, from a sudden blurted exclamation to a rapid dart from one place to another, like a bird hopping through the branches. But the earliest of all these swift and 'flirting' movements was a very surprising one given its meaning today: originally, a *flirt* was a scornful, derisive sneer.

In the mid sixteenth century, *flirting* referred to what we would now more likely call 'turning your nose up'; a *flirt* itself, meanwhile, was a jesting, jibing comment or witticism, or else a nit-picking, carping complainer — the kind of comment or commentator that might be accompanied by a mocking, lip-curling sneer. This meaning endured right through to the mid 1600s, when *flirting* finally began to gain its romantic overtones:

> But now our fears tempestuous grow,
> And cast our hopes away;
> Whilst you, regardless of our woe,
> Sit careless at a play:
> Perhaps, to permit some happier man
> To kiss your hand, or flirt your fan,
> With a fa, la, la, la, la . . .

That's a verse from an old sea shanty called 'To all you ladies now at land' said to have been written by an anonymous English sailor during the First Anglo-Dutch War (1652–54). The song provides us with the earliest written evidence of the expression 'to flirt a fan', which once meant simply 'to flutter or quickly open and close a handheld fan'. But if legend is to be believed, the fan in question isn't being used to cool its owner down. It's being used to send a secret romantic message.

Among young Georgian women, hand-held fans were reputedly much more than a mere fashion accessory, and could instead be used to silently convey messages between sweethearts and suitors. Various combinations of fluttering movements or 'flirts' could communicate everything from reciprocation (sliding a closed fan down the chest = 'I love you') to rejection (lowering an open fan so that it pointed at the ground = 'I hate you'). Whether such a standardised 'fan language' was ever actually employed is debatable, but it was nevertheless through the 'flirting' of fans — and the knowing glances of young Georgian romantics — that the word *flirt* began to be associated with love and lust.

This change in meaning was clearly in place by the early eighteenth century, when the playwright John Gay defined a *flirt* as 'one that gives himself all the airs of making love in public' in 1732. Samuel Johnson defined it as 'a pert young hussy' in his *Dictionary of the English Language* in 1755. And by the late eighteenth century, *flirt* was finally starting to be used as a verb, to mean 'to play at courtship' — or, in the words of the *Oxford English Dictionary*, 'to make love without serious intentions'. By the late 1800s, all earlier meanings of the word had begun to die away, so that by the turn of the century the modern meaning of *flirting* had fully established itself in the language. The days of fluttering hand-held fans and glances across ballrooms might be long gone then, but *flirting* remains with us.

Foyer

originally meant 'green room'

Nowadays, we use the word *foyer* to refer to an entranceway or lobby, typically of some grand building like a hotel or theatre. In fact when it first appeared in English in the mid nineteenth century, *foyer* was only ever used in reference to theatres – though not to describe an entranceway or hallway, but the actors' green room, the room backstage in which performers can wait to go on stage, prepare before a performance, and unwind afterwards. So somehow the word *foyer* has managed to make the move from behind the scenes to front of house. And to understand how that happened, we need to focus not on foyers, but on the word *focus* itself.

Focus was the Latin word for a fireplace, a stove or a hearth. Because all three fixtures are central to a household, over time the word *focus* came to be used more figuratively to refer to any crucially important point or facet, a meaning that still survives in English today. In French, however, *focus* went in a different direction. There, *focus* became *foier* sometime around the early twelfth century, and came to be used not just of fireplaces and hearths, but more generally of homes and households, families and domestic life, and ultimately cosy shelters, asylums and refuges. It's probably from there that the word was first applied to a room in a theatre in which performers can wait before heading to the stage, with the change from backstage to front of house following shortly after – perhaps driven by the idea that the plush lobby of a theatre gave the audience a comfortable place to wait without have to spill out into the cold, rainy streets outside.

Over time, the French *foier* became *foyer* and was adopted into English in this theatrical sense – referring first to an actors' green room, then to the lobby of a theatre – in the mid nineteenth century. Soon it began to be used much more loosely to refer to any grand entranceway or concourse and it's in this sense that the word is most familiar to English speakers today.

But one question remains: why is a green room called a *green room*? The answer to that is the subject of much debate and theatrical folklore. One theory is that it refers to the grass that would once have covered the stage of early open-air theatres. Another claims that travelling players performing at Stratford-upon-Avon had nowhere suitable to change, and so used the local council chambers or 'Agreeing Room'. A much less inventive idea is that the original green room might have been literally that: a room decorated or furnished in a calming shade of green, to rest the actors' eyes from the glare of the stage lights. Or perhaps the term refers to anxious actors literally turning green while they battled to overcome stage-fright in the nervous moments before a performance? If so, it's probably best that that stays backstage . . .

G-string

originally meant 'loincloth'

To the musically uninitiated, overhearing a conversation between two guitarists or string-players about loose G-strings (or, even worse, tight G-strings) might raise a few eyebrows. But those G-strings aren't *those* G-strings of course, rather the strings on musical instruments — namely the highest on a double bass, the third on a cello, viola or guitar, and the fourth and lowest on a violin — that are tuned to the note G.

Musical G-strings like these don't concern us here, though. Instead, we're talking about the wearable ones, which were first described in print in the late 1800s. Back then they were called *geestrings* and, it will come as little surprise to learn, were quite different from the ones we know today:

The Navajo boys are plunging and splashing in the tepid bath . . . Around each boy's waist is the tight 'geestring' from which a single strip of cloth runs between the limbs from front to back – these two articles never being removed from the person in the presence of another.

– John Hanson Beadle, *Western Wilds and the Men Who Redeem Them* (1877)

Although it's clear from that description that this is where the modern G-string takes its name, the original G-string – or rather, the *geestring* – was a Native American loincloth. But why was it called a *geestring* at all?

There are several theories, but frustratingly none is entirely reliable. One claims that the strap forming the basis of this loincloth might have resembled a capital letter G, but that idea seems unlikely (not to mention uncomfortable). Another explanation is that it perhaps resembled a cowboy's whip: the command *gee* has been used to urge on a horse since the seventeenth century at least, while *string* was nineteenth-century slang for a horsewhip. But this theory too seems relatively unlikely (not to mention equally uncomfortable). Maybe 'gee' is a corruption of the Navajo word for 'day', *jí*, implying that the *geestring* was worn only during the daytime and removed at night? Again, it's a nice idea but there's little evidence to support it (besides which, *jí* is pronounced more like 'chay' than it is 'gee'). Instead, perhaps the most likely explanation here is also the most obvious: *geestring* is an abbreviation.

One explanation claims that the 'gee' of *geestring* could be a euphemistic abbreviation of 'groin', a word that might not have been too welcome in print in the mid nineteenth century. But a more plausible idea is that the original *geestring* was in fact a 'girdle-string':

> A very few inches of rag constituted the whole of their drapery; their hair, in long matted stripes, fell in front to the same length as behind, covering the eyes, mouth and chin. Their arms were a small hatchet, stuck in their girdle-string, and a bow of above six feet in height, with two long-bladed arrows.
>
> — 'Elephant-Shooting in Ceylon',
> *Fraser's Magazine* (1846)

This account of a nineteenth-century elephant hunt in Sri Lanka puts weight behind the idea that the 'gee' of *geestring* — and, ultimately, the G of *G-string* — is an abbreviation of *girdle*. But without further evidence it's impossible to say anything with any certainty.

No matter the origin, by the late 1800s the spelling *G-string* (perhaps influenced by its musical cousin) first began to appear. By the 1930s and 40s, it had all but replaced the earlier *gee–* spelling, and the word has remained unchanged ever since.

Garbage

originally meant 'entrails'

Porpoise furmenty. Viper soup. Cockentrice (that's a boiled rooster sewn onto the back end of a suckling pig, in case you didn't know). With dishes like this, frankly it's a brave chef that takes on any recipe from a medieval cookery book – but when the recipe in question goes by the fairly unappetising title of 'garbage', you're on your own:

> Garbage:
> Take fair garbages of chickens, as the head, the feet, the livers, and the gizzards; wash them clean, and cast them in a fair pot, and cast thereto fresh broth of beef or else of mutton, and let it boil.

The cookery book that this recipe comes from was compiled in the early 1400s, when the word *garbage* had less to do with general rubbish and waste material, and more to do with – well, the waste material from butchered animals.

Originally, *garbage* was another word for what we might now call 'offal' or 'entrails', namely the internal parts of an animal carcass that are less apt for eating than the rest of the meat. Precisely where the word itself comes from is a mystery, although the *Oxford English Dictionary* suggests that like many ancient culinary terms, it was likely borrowed from French not long after the Norman Conquest. If that's the case, then *garbage* might derive from *garbe* or *jarbe*, an Old French word for a sheaf or bundle of cereal stalks bound together ready for threshing – and because threshing involves the separation of usable material from the waste (more on that in a moment), it is easy to see from where the association with culinary waste material might have developed.

Whether this etymological theory is correct or not, the use of *garbage* to refer to guts and entrails remained in place in English right through to the late nineteenth century, when the broader meaning of 'refuse' or 'worthless material' finally replaced it. This more general sense first appeared in the late sixteenth century, with the Elizabethan pamphleteer Thomas Nashe warning 'booksellers and stationers' as far back as 1592 to avoid letting their 'shops be infected with any such goose giblets or stinking garbage as the jigs of newsmongers'. But this story doesn't end here . . .

Garble

originally meant 'to separate the good from the bad'

So *garbage* was originally animal entrails, and through association with things that usually are thrown away, eventually
came to mean 'refuse' or 'rubbish'. The problem with that,
however, is that offal and animal entrails are far from useless – as that albeit grim-sounding recipe for medieval *garbage*
illustrates. In fact, so long as you're happy to eat boiled
chickens' heads, garbage of the culinary kind can be used to
make quite a hearty meal, which leaves etymologists with a
problem: what was it that helped push the word *garbage* from
meaning 'not top quality but still usable material' to 'waste
material only good enough to be discarded'? The answer to
that is probably the word *gurble*.

Garble is thought to be derived via Italian from an old
Arabic word, *gharbala*, meaning 'to sift', which in turn is probably based on the Latin word for a sieve, *cribrum*. When
garbling made its first appearance in English in the late fifteenth century this meaning was still in tact, as it essentially
referred to the removal of lower-quality or waste material. In
that sense, it was used specifically in reference to powdered
spices, which would be sieved and sifted – that is, *garbled* –
to remove any tough husks and shells and leave a fine, soft

powder behind. Confusingly, this harder, grittier material was also known as the *garble*, and it is thought that through confusion with this that the word *garbage* began to be associated with useless, waste material only fit to be thrown away. (The modern English word for the coarser material left in a sieve, incidentally, is *cribble*, which is another derivative of the Latin *cribrum*.)

By the early 1600s, however, the verb *garble* was beginning to be used more generally to mean 'to take the pick of something', or 'to sift or weed out anything undesirable'. By the Victorian era, the expression 'garbling the coinage' had emerged, which referred to the somewhat shady practice among moneylenders of melting down any new, unworn coins that came into their possession and returning the more tired, worn down coins back into circulation – but it's not just coins and spices that could be *garbled*.

Facts and statistics, legal documents, items of correspondence, formal documents and all manner of other data and material could likewise be manipulated or 'garbled' so that only its most positive facets were made clear. It was this selective perversion of the truth that eventually led to the word *garble* coming to mean 'to distort' or 'to misrepresent', and by extension, 'to speak incoherently', and eventually it was this meaning that replaced all others in the language.

Girl

originally referred to girls and boys

Some of the changes and semantic sidesteps that the words in our language have undergone are unusual, but not unreasonable. The development from a word meaning 'animal entrails' to a word meaning 'waste material', for instance, isn't too outlandish, nor is the change from 'removing waste material' to 'misrepresenting the facts'. Put the two meanings side by side and you can see how one might develop into the other.

But then you find out that *girls* used to be boys, and suddenly nothing makes sense any more.

Back when it first appeared in the language in the early 1300s, *girl* was gender-neutral. (As was *man*, for that matter, but perhaps more on that later.) So when Chaucer mentioned 'the yonge gerles of the diocise' in the prologue to the *Canterbury Tales* (*c.* 1387), what he really meant was 'all the young children of the diocese'. Likewise, when William Langland mentioned a Latin grammatical textbook called 'Gramer for Girles' in his narrative poem *Piers Plowman* (*c.* 1376), he was referring to a grammar book written for all children. And it's fair to say that the author of this anonymous fifteenth-century guide to young people's manners and etiquette (translated from Middle English) wasn't just picking on girls:

> Gaze not on the walls with thine eyes,
> Far nor near, low nor high . . .
> Nor delve thou never thy nostril,
> With thumb or finger as a young girl.
> — *The Babees' Book, or A Little Report of How*
> *Young People Should Behave* (*c.* 1475)

Frustratingly, no one is quite sure where the word *girl* and its original ungendered meaning comes from. Several different theories (of differing levels of plausibility) have been suggested over the years, pointing to everything from an Old English word for an item of children's clothing, *gyrela*, to the Latin word *garrulus*, meaning 'talkative' or 'chatty'. None is entirely watertight however, and ultimately the word *girl* remains a true etymological mystery. But what about the change from gender-neutral to gender-specific? Do we know what happened there?

Girl began to be used exclusively to refer to female children around the early 1400s. By the turn of the century this meaning had taken over and consigned the older gender-neutral one to the history books – and tellingly, it was around this time that the word *boy* likewise began to be used all but exclusively of male children.

Boy is thought to have been borrowed into English from French in the early thirteenth century. It originally referred to a man of lowly birth or social status, or else a male servant or slave (one theory even claims that it might have derived from an Old French word, *embuie*, meaning 'held in fetters'). But as time went by, *boy* came to be used much more generally to refer to a male child, and consequently it began to encroach on the original meaning of *girl*. In response, *girl* had to restrict its meaning to make room for *boy* – or else risk disappearing from the language altogether. After co-existing for a time, eventually the two words became fixed on the two opposite genders, and we have had *girls* and *boys* ever since.

Glamour

was originally magic

What comes to mind when you think of the word *glamour*? Hollywood icons? Yachts in Monte Carlo harbour? Reflexive pronouns? Things really don't come more glamorous than that – quite literally, in fact, as *glamour* and *grammar* are actually a lot more closely related to one another than they might appear.

Derived via Latin from the Greek *grammatike*, meaning 'pertaining to letters', the word *grammar* was borrowed into English from French in the early fourteenth century. At that time, it was only used to refer to the rules that governed the structure of Latin (it wasn't until the mid 1500s that it came to be used of English) and because being well versed in Latin was seen as indicative of a good education, by the Middle Ages *grammar* had come to be associated with any subject considered unique to the learned classes and beyond the comprehension of the relatively less well educated. Consequently, treatises on all kinds of different subjects came to be known as 'grammars', and the term gradually began to entail everything from geography to geometry, alchemy to astrology – and through association with them, magic and demonology.

The association between grammar and occultic subjects like these still survives in a handful of fairly obscure words such as *gramary*, a fifteenth-century word for a knowledge of mysticism and occult magic, and *grimoire*, another word book of spells or incantations (which literally means 'grammar' in French). But this meaning also survives in the glamorous world of *glamour*.

Glamour began life as a Scots dialect word, formed, straight-forwardly enough, from a local corruption of *grammar*. It was grammar's mystical rather than linguistic connotations that were carried through to Scots, however, so that when *glamour* first appeared in the language in the mid 1700s it was used to mean 'magic', 'enchantment', or 'bewitchment'. In this context, it was more often than not used in the old expression 'to cast a glamour over someone', which essentially meant 'to bewitch' or 'enchant':

> Like Belzie [Beelzebub] when he nicks a Witch,
> Wha sells her Saul she may be rich;
> He finding this the Bait to damn her,
> Casts o'er her Een his Cheating glamour.
>
> — Allan Ramsay,
> 'The Rise and Fall of Stocks' (1720)

The word *glamour* remained confined to Scots English until the nineteenth century, when its use finally began to spread (due in no small part to the popularity of Scottish poets and writers like Ramsay, Robert Burns and Sir Walter Scott). At the same time, its meaning began to broaden so that by the mid 1800s, *glamour* was being used to refer to any alluring quality or charm that has the ability to entice and enchant someone, and by the turn of the century it had gained its contemporary meaning of attractiveness, stylishness and glitziness.

Grammar, meanwhile, eventually lost its association with black magic and enchantment, and returned to being associated merely with language rules and structures. And you can't get much more glamorous than that.

Grin

originally meant 'snarl'

A few pages back, we found out that *flirting* with someone in the Middle Ages involved sneering at them contemptuously. Hardly the best way to break the romantic ice, really, but surely you're on much safer ground just smiling politely? Perhaps. But *grinning* is a different matter entirely.

Grin is the modern descendant of an Old English word, *grennian*, that essentially meant 'to bear your teeth'. Although we tend to use it today to mean 'to smile broadly', originally *grin* had connotations of pain, anguish and anger, and the grimacing, contorted expressions that accompany unpleasant feelings or riled emotions:

> There are some jesters who know of no other means of exciting mirth but to make wry faces, and distort their mouth, and scowl with their eyes . . . in the devil's court, to excite to laughter their envious Lord. If anyone says or does well, they cannot by any means look that way with the direct eye of a good heart, but wink in another direction . . . These are their own prophets, foretelling their own doom. They foreshadow beforehand how they themselves will later be terrified

by the grinning of hideous devils, and how they themselves will twist and distort their features, grimacing
from the great anguish of the pains of Hell.

— *Ancrene Riwle* (*c.* 1225)

The *Ancrene Riwle* was an early-thirteenth-century manual
(translated from its original Middle English here) that was
written for young women looking to live the solitary life
of an anchoress. Its author is unknown, but whoever they
were, they clearly took a strong dislike to jesters and come-
dians — here intended to represent the sin of envy — who
poke fun at good and honourable people. Their opinions on
comedy aside, the author makes the negative connotations of
the word *grinning* very clear: the 'hideous devils' tormenting
the jesters in the bowels of Hell aren't smiling sweetly, but
grinning malevolently.

Over time, this meaning of *grin* began to weaken so that
by the early 1500s it was being used to describe merely a
forced, faked or otherwise unnatural smile. From there, it
came to be applied to embarrassed and foolish smiles, and
finally by the time Charles Dickens coined the phrase 'to
grin from ear to ear' in *Barnaby Rudge* (1841), to broad and
unrestrained smiles.

The original meaning of *grin* along with its connotations of pain and anguish largely fell out of use in the
late 1600s, replaced in most contexts by the word as it is

today. Nevertheless clues to its origins remain in a handful of stock phrases and expressions that still survive in the language. 'To grin on the wrong side of the mouth', for instance, means 'to laugh with an ugly grimace' according to the *English Dialect Dictionary* (1900). 'To grin and bear it' or 'to grin and abide' has been used to mean 'to patiently endure something unpleasant' or 'to acknowledge your fate' since the late eighteenth century. And, as the English lexicographer Francis Grose explained in his *Dictionary of the Vulgar Tongue* (1785), 'grinning in a glass case' might once have been precisely the kind of fate an eighteenth-century criminal would have to acknowledge:

> To grin in a glass case; to be anatomised for murder: the skeletons of many criminals are preserved in glass cases, at the surgeon's hall.
>
> – Francis Grose, *A Classical Dictionary of the Vulgar Tongue* (1785)

Hallucinate

originally meant 'deceive'

According to Jack London, there are two types of drunks. On the one hand, there is the man who 'even when most pleasantly jingled', remains physically solid. 'He walks straight and naturally, never staggers nor falls, and knows just where he is and what he is doing,' London explained. And on the other hand, there is the drunk who becomes wholly incapacitated:

> There is the man whom we all know, stupid, unimaginative, whose brain is bitten numbly by numb maggots; who walks generously with wide-spread, tentative legs, falls frequently in the gutter, and who sees, in the extremity of his ecstasy, blue mice and pink elephants. He is the type that gives rise to the jokes in the funny papers.
>
> — Jack London, *John Barleycorn* (1913)

Hey, we've all been there. Drunks and drunkards have been hallucinating pink elephants since the late nineteenth century — it's thought the phrase first gained currency via the great American showman P. T. Barnum, who to considerable publicity and promotion, purchased a legendary white elephant from the king of Burma in 1884. Despite paying an eye-watering $200,000 (equivalent to over $5 million today), Barnum's white elephant unfortunately turned out to be nothing of the sort. As one newspaper, the *St Paul Daily Globe*, cuttingly reported at the time: 'It has a few pinkish spots on its trunk and ears, and that is all. The white elephant is simply a sick elephant.' *Pink elephants*, then, are apparently nothing more than hallucinations – but Barnum himself had literally been *hallucinated*.

Hallucinate derives from a Latin word, *alucinari*, that was variously used to mean 'to daydream', 'to chatter unthinkingly', or 'to wander around idly'. But when it first appeared in English in the early 1600s, *hallucinate* originally meant 'to deceive' or 'to hoodwink'. These early definitions are clearly based around the notion of someone credulously falling for something imaginary or invented, or else signing up to some fantasised or romanticised ideal. But given that the word's Latin root could also be used of prattling, digressive speech, it's possible that *hallucinating* also once had connotations of being duped by a chattering salesman, or by a con artist's convincing patter.

By the eighteenth century, this meaning had broadened so that *hallucinate* was being used to mean 'to make a mistake' or 'to blunder'; Samuel Johnson defined a *hallucination* as an 'error' or 'folly' in his *Dictionary of the English Language* (1755). By the nineteenth century, this sense was starting to disappear and *hallucinating* was beginning to have less to do with falling for something non-existent, and more to do with seeing or imagining something that isn't actually there. Webster's *American Dictionary* (1828) labelled Johnson's definition of *hallucination* as 'little used', and in its place defined the word as 'erroneous imagination', of the kind that might 'arise from some imaginary or mistaken idea'. 'Similar hallucinations', Webster explained, 'occur in reverie' – which might include the odd pink elephant.

Handicap

was originally a method of securing a deal

There's another old story that claims the word *handicap* derives from wounded soldiers returning home from battle with devastating injuries that prevented them from going back to their day jobs. In desperation, they were left with little recourse but to beg on the streets – their caps literally held in their hands, to catch the donations of passers-by.

It's an ingenious story. It's just a shame that it's completely untrue, not least because this would more likely have given us the word 'capihand' rather than *handicap*. Instead, the true origin of *handicap* lies in *hand-in-cap*, an old method of trading goods dating back to the early Middle Ages, in which it was not the caps that were placed in the hands, but the hands that were placed in the caps.

Imagine two traders are looking to exchange goods, but are unsure about the relative value of the items they're looking to swap. In a 'hand-in-cap' trade, they would turn to a third party — essentially a kind of umpire — who would take a look at the items up for exchange and assess their value. If he thought there were any kind of discrepancy between the two, he would come up with a price (referred to as the 'odds', or the 'boot') that the owner of the cheaper lot would have to add into the exchange to make it fair. Next, out comes the cap.

The umpire, having given his assessment of the exchange, would then hold out his upturned cap. Both of the traders would take a few loose coins from their pockets and, holding the cash in their hands, would place their hands inside the cap. If they agreed to the exchange, they'd drop their money into it. If they didn't, they'd keep it in their hands.

If both traders agreed, the exchange would go ahead as planned and the umpire would get to keep whatever change had been thrown in the cap — his reward for making an acceptable valuation. If neither of the traders agreed, no exchange would take place, and the umpire would get nothing — his penalty for making an unfair or inaccurate assessment.

And if only one trader agreed, they would get to retrieve their cash from the cap, no exchange would take place, and the umpire would still get nothing. Whatever the outcome, the umpire was always incentivised to come up with as fair an exchange as possible, and the trade would only go ahead once everyone was happy.

But how does an obscure medieval trade system lead us to the word *handicap* as we have it today? Well, it was the notion of assessing the value of something that eventually led to the first *handicap* horse races in the mid eighteenth century, in which an adjudicator is brought in to assess the quality of the horses taking part. Stronger horses are laden down with weights to hamper their speed and make for a fairer race overall – and it's from there that the use of *handicap* to refer to something that hampers or encumbers ordinary activity eventually emerged in the late 1800s.

Hanky-panky

originally meant 'sleight of hand'

In 1847, a Victorian journalist and humorist named Albert Richard Smith published a comic novel called *The Life and*

Adventures of Christopher Tadpole, a Dickensian tale full of comedic misadventures and colourful characters – one of whom, encountered by Christopher on a country road in the middle of nowhere, is a professor of magic called Mr Swaby:

> 'So; I place that cork ball there. I put it in my hand, and I swallow it. Presto! it is gone: and I produce it from my ear.'
> 'Why; that's conjuring,' observed Christopher.
> 'Necromancy, my dear Sir – the hanky-panky of the ancients.'
>
> — Albert Richard Smith, *The Life and Adventures of Christopher Tadpole* (1847)

Strictly speaking, *necromancy* is prognostication through contact with the dead, but it's being used here in more general terms (as it very often is) as a synonym for black magic or sorcery. But what about *hanky-panky*? To modern audiences, *hanky-panky* has sexual overtones, so describing anything to do with dealings with the dead as 'hanky-panky' might sound bizarre at best – and downright illegal at worst. But happily things aren't quite as morally questionable as they might appear.

The word *hanky-panky* is only around as old as Smith's novel: the *Oxford English Dictionary* has unearthed its earliest record in an 1841 edition of *Punch*, the satirical magazine to which Smith was one of the earliest contributors. Back then, *hanky-panky* meant simply 'trickery' or 'sleight of hand' – a *hanky-panky bloke* was a professional magician in Victorian theatrical slang – and it's in this sense that the word appears here in Smith's novel.

As for where the word derives from, no one is entirely sure. A common theory is that it refers to the coloured handkerchiefs or 'hankies' used by conjurors in magic tricks, to which 'panky' might have been added for no other reason that to make a ludicrous rhyme. But calling a handkerchief a 'hankie' is apparently a later nineteenth-century invention, all but unheard of around the time that *hanky-panky* first emerged.

Instead, *hanky-panky* is likely to be a fanciful corruption of *hocus-pocus*, a conjuror's exclamation that began life in the seventeenth century as a byword for a magician or entertainer. Predictably, no one is sure where *hocus-pocus* comes from too, although a popular theory is that it might be a ludicrous corruption of a chain of words lifted from the Latin Catholic Mass, *hoc est corpus meum*, or 'this is my body'.

Hanky-panky might have originally meant 'magic' then, but this meaning was quick to advance. Through association with trickery and sleight of hand, by the later 1800s it had come to be used of double-dealing or underhand, swindling tricks or deceptions; and through association with those, by the 1930s it had come to refer to romantic indiscretion and sexual dalliances. It's this meaning that has survived through to modern English – and which makes interpreting extracts like that from Smith's novel a somewhat thorny business.

Hat-trick

was originally a practical joke

Just about any sport you choose to play (or choose to avoid playing, should you prefer reading books) will have its own version of a *hat-trick*, each of which corresponds to some kind of three-in-a-row achievement. In goal-scoring games like football and hockey, it refers to three goals scored by a single player in a single game. In rugby, it's three tries scored in one game. In baseball, it's three home runs in a single game. Score three consecutive bullseyes in darts, knock three players out of a game of poker with one hand, or even play three seven-letter words in a row in a game of Scrabble, and you'll score a *hat-trick*. But the earliest of all sporting *hat-tricks* wasn't any of these – and the earliest meaning of the word itself had nothing to do with sport at all.

The first sport to have a *hat-trick* was cricket. In cricketing terms, a *hat-trick* involves a single player taking three wickets, and thereby dismissing three opposing batsmen with three consecutive balls. It's an understandably rare feat, but is by no means impossible: in a century-and-a-half of Test cricket, there have been forty-one recorded hat-tricks, the first in 1879, the most recent in 2014.

So why a 'hat' trick? According to a late-nineteenth-century dictionary of *Slang and its Analogues Past and Present* (1893), scoring a *hat-trick* in cricket was 'held to entitle the bowler to a new hat at the cost of the club'. Another explanation claims that it alludes to the very first sporting hat-trick on record, when in 1858 the English bowler H. H. Stephenson took three wickets with three consecutive balls, and so impressed the crowd that a hat was sent round to raise a collection for him. But however true (or untrue) these stories might be, there was an even earlier *hat-trick* that was not only an actual trick, but unquestionably involved an actual hat.

The earliest record of the phrase *hat-trick* that we know about comes from a collection of mid-nineteenth-century parlour games first published the year before Stephenson's hat-trick, in 1857:

> The Hat Trick. Fill a small glass with water, cover it with a hat, and profess your readiness to drink it without touching the hat. Put your head under the table, make a noise as if drinking, rise and wipe your lips. The company, thinking you have drunk the water, one of them will certainly take up the hat to see.

As soon as the hat is removed, take up the glass and drink the contents. 'There,' say you, 'you see I have not touched the hat!'

– George Frederick Pardon,
Parlour Pastimes: A Repertoire (1857)

A variation of this *hat-trick* – a mid-nineteenth-century prank that perhaps began as a wager or a practical joke among drinkers – was described even earlier than this in a collection of *Home Amusements* compiled in the early 1850s by an anonymous author going by the name of 'Peter Puzzlewell'. In his description, this trick was known only as 'the two-fold meaning', but Puzzlewell's description adds that whoever is playing the trick should 'get under the table, [and] give three knocks', and it's that knocking that will magically trigger the transformation above.

Could it be that Puzzlewell's prank is actually the original *hat-trick*? It's certainly possible, as it not only accounts for the name but also its association with a somewhat remarkable set of three. Either way, it is highly likely that the popularity of pranks and tricks like these helped to establish the phrase *hat-trick* in the mid-nineteenth-century vernacular, from where it was only a short sidestep into the sporting slang of the day.

Heartache

was originally heartburn

Seven lines into the famous 'To be or not to be' speech in Act III of Shakespeare's *Hamlet*, the melancholy prince wrestles with a dejected feeling common to everyone who has ever loved, lost or grieved:

> . . . To die, to sleep —
> No more — and by a sleep to say we end
> The heartache and the thousand natural shocks
> That flesh is heir to. 'Tis a consummation
> Devoutly to be wished. To die, to sleep —
> To sleep — perchance to dream. Ay, there's the rub.

What a shame, then, that Hamlet wasn't around in the early ninth century, when an Anglo-Saxon textbook of medical treatments and cure-alls called *Bald's Leechbook* was compiled. Divided into three volumes — the first arranged anatomically from head to toe, the second and third covering all manner of other injuries and conditions from spider bites to demonic possession — the *Leechbook* is renowned for outlining a number of remarkably advanced and effective remedies. It includes a relatively informed method of amputating a limb, advocates what is essentially plastic surgery for treatment of a hare-lip, and includes a recipe for a medicinal eye salve that in 2015 was found to be effective in killing antibiotic-resistant MRSA. And in between all of those, Bald (who, according to the inscription at least, was the owner rather than author of the book) found the time to include no fewer than three different cures for heartache:

> With heartache, boil a handful of rue in oil, and add an ounce of aloes, rub the body with that. It stilleth the sore . . . For heartache again, take githrife [fennel-flower], boil it in milk, give to drink for six days . . . Take pepper, cumin, and costmary, rub them into beer or into water, administer to drink.

Aside from drowning your sorrows in a glass of warmed and spiced beer, you'd be forgiven for thinking that there's little here that might help to mend a broken heart. But that's because Bald's *heartache* and Hamlet's *heartache* — and, for that matter, our *heartache* today — are not the same thing.

In Old English, *heartache* was heartburn, the dyspeptic burning sensation in the chest or abdomen caused by drops of acid escaping the stomach and burning the inside of the oesophagus. (Needless to say, that wasn't one of the 'thousand natural shocks' that Hamlet had in mind.) This purely medical meaning of *heartache* remained in use in the language right through to the nineteenth century, at which point it was finally all but replaced by the more figurative sense of 'emotional anguish' or 'heartbreak', which had first emerged in the late sixteenth century. But in that case . . .

Heartburn

was originally lust

. . . if *heartache* was originally heartburn, what are we supposed to make of this?:

The young women of thy land,
Fair of face and soft of hand,
And bright of hue, of speech glad,
In haste shall I set apart as messengers;
Do thou send out against these men
Those who can brew heartburn
With pleasure, and beauty, and body, and deceit,
Amorously, with small speech,
To turn them from God's awe.

— 'The Story of Genesis and Exodus'
(*c.* 1250)

This is an extract (translated from the original Middle English) from a poetic retelling of the opening books of the Bible written in the mid thirteenth century. Here, the prophet Balaam is advising the king of the Moabites, Balak, how best to defeat the Israelites, and hatches a plan to have all the most beautiful young women of Balak's kingdom sent out to tempt the Israelite men. Unable to resist their charms and 'small speech' (i.e. flattery), Balaam explains that the Israelites will yield to temptation, and their adultery and debauchery will attract the wrath of God.

Needless to say, giving all the Israelites *heartburn* is not part of Balaam's plan – the God of the Old Testament might be a vengeful god, but indigestion is seemingly a step too far. So what does the author mean by tempting the Israelites with 'the young women of thy land . . . who can brew heartburn'? Well, back in the mid 1200s when this poem was written, *heartburn* did not mean what it means today, but instead meant something like 'intense passion', 'desire' or 'lustfulness'; the heart was seen as the seat of all human emotion, and so a 'burning' in the heart implied a burning, passionate love or lust.

By the early Middle Ages, however, all that had changed:

For þe hertbryne. Tak wormode & sethe it in water & drynk it.

That is an extract from a fifteenth-century medical textbook, *Liber de Diversis Medicinis* or 'The Book of Diverse Medicines', that recommends a draught of boiled wormwood as a medical treatment for heartburn. This cure wouldn't have helped the Israelites, of course: unlike *heartache*, which remained in use as another name for indigestion right through to the nineteenth century, the romantic connotations of *heartburn* did not last long and had already disappeared by the time this textbook was compiled in the mid 1400s. *Heartburn* has remained purely a medical term ever since.

Hijinks

was originally a drinking game

Let's play a quick game. What do these words have in common: *hijinks, abcoulomb, student, defeated, Tuvalu, nope, Ghibelline*. A *Ghibelline* was a supporter of the Holy Roman emperor's authority in medieval Italy, incidentally, and an *abcoulomb* is a unit of electrical charge. But you really don't need to know that to figure out the answer. Still thinking? Have a bit more time, but don't worry — it's just a little bit of linguistic *hijinks*.

Hijinks, or *high jinks*, has been used to mean 'fun and games' or 'boisterous horseplay' since the mid nineteenth century, but the word itself has a lengthy history and originally referred to a much more specific bit of horseplay than that.

Jink is an old Scots word for a sudden or swift movement, particularly one used to evade someone or something threatening. As a verb, it can be used to mean 'to dodge', 'to move to and fro', 'to escape notice', or even 'to make an unobtrusive entrance', while *to jink the school* once meant 'to play truant' and *to give the jink* meant 'to give someone the slip'. Seemingly, no matter what the context might be, *jink* has clear connotations of eluding or otherwise getting the better of someone. So if those are the 'jinks', why are they 'high'?

The fact that *jinks* appears to be a Scots word has led to suggestions that the '*hi-*' of *hijinks* might be another Scots word, *hy*, meaning 'haste' or 'speed'. Alternatively, it could just as likely be the word *high*, here implying some sense of impressiveness or quality. Whatever the correct interpretation, the two words first came together in the late seventeenth century – when they were originally the name of a raucous drinking game:

Our Batt can dance, play at high jinks with dice,
At any primitive, orthodoxal vice.
Shooting the wild mare, tumbling the young wenches,
Drinking all night, and sleeping on the benches.
    – John Speed, 'Batt Upon Batt' (1680)

Crikey, those seventeenth-century drinkers sure knew how to have a good time. Although it's likely the name *high jinks* was used of a number of different games, each with different rules and outcomes, dice were apparently always involved. Likewise, the player who lost, scored lowest, or otherwise failed to respond correctly to the number rolled was made to pay some kind of forfeit, either by downing their drink, or paying the bar tab:

> The frolicsome company had begun to practise the ancient and now forgotten pastime of high jinks. This game was played in several different ways. Most frequently the dice were thrown by the company, and those upon whom the lot fell were obliged to assume and maintain for a time a certain fictitious character, or to repeat a certain number of fescennine *[obscene]* verses in a particular order. If they departed from the characters assigned, or if their memory proved treacherous in the repetition, they incurred forfeits, which were either compounded for by swallowing an additional bumper or by paying a small sum towards the reckoning.
>
> – Sir Walter Scott, *Guy Mannering* (1815)

Hijinks remained in use as the name of a drinking game right through the mid 1800s. But as the game continued to fall out of fashion, the meaning of the word altered and *hijinks* began instead to be used more generally to refer to fun and games of any kind. Which brings us back to where we started.

Have you worked it out yet? The answer is that *hijinks*, *abcoulomb*, *student* and all those other words each begin with three consecutive letters of the alphabet: HIJ, ABC, STU and so on. Well done if you got it right – you've earned yourself a drink.

Hussy

originally meant 'housewife'

When they first appeared back in the early Old English period, the words *husband* and *wife* were not the matching pair they are today. *Wife* simply meant 'woman' (in fact, *woman* itself comes from Old English *wifman*, literally 'woman-man') while the word *husband* applied merely to the male head of a household, not necessarily a male spouse. *Husband* itself literally means 'house-dweller', although it is thought to have its roots in an even older Scandinavian word that literally referred to someone responsible for working and cultivating the land around a house. 'I now pronounce you land-cultivator and woman' just doesn't have the same ring to it as 'husband and wife' really.

All of that makes the etymological counterpart of *husband* not *wife* but *housewife*, a term that likewise began to emerge for the female head of a household in the early thirteenth century. From there, both *husband* and *housewife* went on to gain broader connotations of management, economy and organisation: the title *husbandman* is still used today in relation to a farmer or someone skilled in *husbandry*, while in the seventeenth century the word *housewife* even came to be used as a verb, meaning 'to economise', 'to skilfully manage finances' or 'to eke out a supply'. But while *husband* went on to lose all its connections to the household and, by the fifteenth century at least, became all but exclusively attached to a male spouse, *housewife* has retained all of its domestic associations – and, in that sense, eventually inspired a somewhat unexpected derivative.

Despite its derogatory connotations, the word *hussy* is a contraction of *housewife*. When it first appeared in the early 1500s, it too referred to the female head of a household, and at one time even enjoyed the same connotations of thriftiness and skill with money. A *hussy*, in other words, was a domestic goddess:

All this while I had no sufficient evidence of her guilt . . . nor did I find she had been extravagant

in her expenses while I was abroad; but jealousie, as
the wise man says, is the wrath of a man; her being
so good a hussy of what money I had left her, gave
my distemper'd fancy an opinion that she had been
maintain'd by other people.

— Daniel Defoe, *Colonel Jack* (1722)

All that began to change in the mid 1600s. Around that time
hussy began to be used more typically of strong, characterful,
rustic countrywomen, and eventually — though somewhat
unfairly — with women of lower social standings. Once there,
it began to shed all its positive connotations, so that by the
late eighteenth century a *hussy* was no longer a well-organised
housewife, but a disreputable, dissolute young woman. The
transformation was complete, and the word has remained
unchanged in English ever since — and frankly, 'I now pronounce you husband and hussy' sounds even worse than
what we had before.

Inmate

originally meant 'lodger'

It's hardly a big surprise: an *inmate* is literally a 'mate' with whom you are held 'in' somewhere. A fellow confinee, in other words. Someone with whom you're sharing living quarters. Given that that has been the word's meaning ever since it first appeared in the language in the late sixteenth century, you might wonder what *inmate* has done to deserve a place on this list. Well, although the meaning of the word might not have changed much, precisely what the 'mates' in question are 'in' has.

Since the mid 1800s, *inmate* has come to be used almost exclusively of people held somewhere against their will or better judgement, and in particular of those who are confined somewhere as punishment or for their own good. Today, it is seldom seen outside of the context of prisons, but over the years has been applied to all kinds of other institutions where you might find yourself interned or institutionalised, including everything from hospitals to mental asylums.

Historically, however, the word was used much more generally and an *inmate* was merely someone with whom you shared a dwelling or living quarters. In that sense, it was essentially a synonym of what we'd now call a *lodger* or *tenant*, as in this 1589 Act of Parliament:

> From and after the feast of All Saints next coming, there shall not be any inmate, or more families or households than one, dwelling or inhabiting in any one cottage . . . upon paine that every owner or occupier of any such cottage . . . shall forfeit and lose to the lord of the leet *[a court of local disputes]* . . . the summe of ten shillings of lawfull mony of England.
>
> — The Husbandry Act
> (31 Elizabeth c.7, 1589)

The fact that an *inmate* was once just a paying lodger has even led to the suggestion that at its very earliest it would have referred to an 'inn-mate' – namely someone who rents a room in a hostel or guesthouse – rather than just an 'in-mate', but without evidence that theory is all but impossible to prove. Nevertheless, the original meaning of the word endured for the next three centuries: Samuel Johnson's *Dictionary* (1755) defined *inmates* as merely 'those that be admitted to dwell for their money jointly with another man', while Noah Webster's *American Dictionary of the English Language* (1828) referred to 'a person who lodges or dwells in the same house with another, occupying different rooms, but using the same door for passing in and out of the house'. But things had begun to change by the end of the nineteenth century.

An extended edition of Webster's dictionary, the *International Dictionary of the English Language* (1890), pointed out that the word *inmate* was now being used especially of 'one of the occupants of an asylum, hospital, or prison' and the word has failed to shake off its associations with incarceration or institutionalisation ever since. Why the change in meaning? It's probably all down to what was happening in society at the time.

The nineteenth century not only saw the reform and establishment of the first regular police forces, but as towns and cities expanded and industrialised, crime rates soared – and so too did the prison population. Transportation and hanging were starting to be seen as less appropriate sentences for minor offences, especially given that imprisonment was cheaper and provided opportunities for reform and penance. Between 1842 and 1877, no fewer than 90 prisons were built or extended in England alone – and as all these changes were enacted, they took the word *inmate* along with them.

The letter J

was originally the letter I

In 1011, an English monk named Byrhtferð of Ramsey, based at Ramsey Abbey in Cambridgeshire, published a scientific manual called the *Enchiridion* (a Latin word for a handbook or manual). Alongside tables of weights and measures and essays on everything from rhetorical tropes to the age of the Earth, Byrhtferð wrote lengthy treatises on numerology and the symbolic significance of letters and numbers – and amidst all of that, he wrote out the earliest record of the English alphabet in history:

A B C D E F G H I K L M N O P Q R S T V X
Y Z & 7 Ᵽ Þ Ð Æ

Clearly, things have changed. For one thing, Byrhtferð's alphabet contains no fewer than twenty-nine letters, rather than twenty-six, thanks to the addition of the ancient runic letters *wynn* (Ᵽ), *thorn* (Þ) and *eth* (Ð), the Anglo-Saxon letter *ash* (Æ, a ligature combining A and E), and both the *ampersand* (&) and so-called *Tironian ond* (7) used to represent the word 'and'. Despite totalling twenty-nine, however, there are some glaring omissions here too. There's no W, which had yet to develop independently from the letter U. For that matter, there's also no U, which had yet to be recognised as a separate letter from V. And there's no J, for good reason – J would not make its first appearance in the language for another five centuries, and even then it would not be the letter J that we recognise and use today.

J is the most recent addition to our alphabet. The origins and ancestors of many of our other letters stretch way back into antiquity (A, for instance, began life more than 3,500 years ago as an Ancient Egyptian hieroglyph representing an ox's head). But J did not begin to emerge until the medieval period, around 700–800 years ago, when it developed from its alphabetical neighbour, I. To I, a tail or 'swash' was added to produce a curled symbol, *J*, whose purpose was merely to represent the last in a chain of Roman numeral Is – so 13 would once have been written *xiij* rather than *xiii*, 23 as *xxiij* not *xxiii*, and so on. Hence at its very earliest, the letter J was essentially just the letter I in disguise.

At that time, I could be used both as a vowel, as it still is today, and as a consonant, in which case it represented a sound known as the 'voiced palatal approximant' (in other words, the 'y' sound in words like *you* and *yet*). This use of I accounts for the likes of *iust* (instead of *just*) and *iustice* (instead of *justice*) cropping up in old documents and inscriptions, and explains why old religious texts and scriptures often talk of *Iesus* and *Ioseph*, rather than 'Jesus' and 'Joseph'.

It's also why Indiana Jones misspells 'Jehovah' in *The Last Crusade*. But I digress.

All that began to change in the early sixteenth century, when along came a Renaissance poet and grammarian named Gian Giorgio Trissino. In his *Epistle on the Letters Recently Added to the Italian Language* (1524), Trissino made a case for using the relatively newly developed I-with-a-swash, J, to represent the consonantal form of I, leaving I as a vowel only. His suggestion proved popular and, once adopted, quickly spread into other European languages before finding its way into English in the late 1500s. By the seventeenth century, *J* had established itself as an entirely new letter of the alphabet, and has remained in use in this way ever since.

Jargon

was originally birdsong

Labyrinthine phone contracts. Cringeworthy business-speak clichés. Obfuscating political speeches. Nowadays, we tend to use the word *jargon* to refer to any impenetrable or otherwise incomprehensible language, intentional or otherwise. But birdsong?

He was al coltissh, ful of ragerye,
And ful of jargon as a flekked pye.
The slakke skyn aboute his nekke shaketh,
Whil that he sang, so chaunteth he and craketh.
– Geoffrey Chaucer,
The Canterbury Tales (*c.* 1387)

These lines are taken from Chaucer's *Merchant's Tale*, written in the late fourteenth century. Here, the ageing and vain lothario January has just joined his twenty-something new bride May in bed on their wedding night, and serenaded her with a song that 'shakes the slack skin around his neck'. In Chaucer's words, January is 'full of jargon like a flecked pie', or magpie – but given the context, you can be fairly sure he's not talking about his new mobile phone contract.

The word *jargon* was borrowed into English from French in the early fourteenth century. It is believed to have begun life as another word for birdsong or the constant wittering or chattering sounds of birds, in which case it was probably originally onomatopoeic and was somehow intended to imitate a chirping or chirruping sound. If that's the case, *jargon* might have an unlikely etymological cousin in *cajole*, which is thought to derive from an Old French word meaning 'to chatter like a jay' and probably originally referred to the act of enticing or 'cajoling' a bird into a cage or trap.

But because birdsong is all but unintelligible to us, it

didn't take long for *jargon* to come to be used of any equally unintelligible chatter or talk. This meaning was already present in French by the time English adopted the word *jargon* in the mid 1300s, and both meanings – birdsong and nonsense talk – arrived in the language around the same time. Here in Chaucer's *Merchant's Tale*, both meanings are being played on simultaneously: January is serenading his wife (albeit not particularly well), but he could just as easily be chattering away inanely and unintelligibly 'like a flecked pie' (i.e. a magpie).

The use of *jargon* as another word for birdsong all but disappeared in the fifteenth century, while its use as another word for prattle or nonsense-speak thrived. By the early sixteenth century, it was being applied to encrypted, symbol-based writing; by the early seventeenth century, it was being used of muddled and hybridised mixtures of languages, and conversations between multilingual speakers that slip from one language to another; and by the mid seventeenth century, the modern sense of language that is (either intentionally or unintentionally) full of technical terminology and esoteric vocabulary finally emerged. A derivative verb, *jargonise*, followed on in the early nineteenth century, while someone who uses jargon in their everyday speech has been called a *jargonist* since the late 1700s.

Jiffy

originally meant 'flash of lightning'

Look the word *jiffy* up in any dictionary, and you'll be told the same thing: origin unknown. The *Oxford English Dictionary*, *Collins Dictionary*, *Chambers Dictionary* and *Merriam-Webster Dictionary*, among countless others, all agree *jiffy* is a mystery. But just because its origin is unknown, doesn't mean that we don't know anything – and according to one theory at least, *jiffy* began life as another word for a flash of lightning.

The earliest record of the word *jiffy* comes from Rudolf Erich Raspe's *Surprising Adventures of Baron Munchausen* (1785), in which the eponymous baron finds himself and all his retinue 'in six jiffies . . . at the rock of Gibraltar'. It's possible that the word *jiffy* was coined by Raspe himself – but that theory is thrown into doubt by this definition:

> JEFFY. It will be done in a jeffy; it will be done in a short space of time, in an instant.

That's an entry from the third edition of Francis Grose's *Classical Dictionary of the Vulgar Tongue*, published in 1796. If *jiffy* was indeed Raspe's invention, could it have caught on successfully enough in the language to warrant a place in

Grose's dictionary – albeit with a slightly different spelling – barely a decade later? It's debatable. Instead, we have to presume that Raspe had picked up the word from elsewhere, but with no earlier record of *jiffy* in print before him, the trail here runs cold. Until we get to this:

> JEFFY. A slang term amongst thieves for lightning.
> It is probable that 'in a jiffy', i.e., in a moment, may
> have originated in this connection, or vice versa.

That's an entry from an 1889 dictionary of *Americanisms Old and New* by the American lexicographer John S. Farmer. An even earlier nineteenth-century dictionary of slang, *Vocabulum, or The Rogue's Lexicon* (1859) compiled by George W. Matsell – New York City's first chief of police, no less – also listed *jeffey*-with-an-extra-E as a slang word for lightning. Could it be that this was the original meaning of *jiffy*?

It's certainly a plausible theory, but by no means a water-tight one. The near 75-year gap between *Baron Munchausen* and Matsell's *Vocabulum* is hard to explain, as is the lack of any mention of lightning in Grose's dictionary, despite him being perhaps the most dedicated slang lexicographer of his day (moreover, *jiffy* was omitted from the two earlier editions of his dictionary, in 1785 and 1788). Alternatively, as the defin-ition above points out, *vice versa* could be true: *jiffy* might have always meant 'an instant', and based on that association came to be used of a flash of lightning in the nineteenth century. Either way, the word had one more trick up its sleeve.

In the early 1900s, the American physicist Gilbert Newton Lewis (known for coining the word *photon*) seized upon the word *jiffy* and gave it a standard scientific definition of 33.3564 picoseconds. One *jiffy*, Lewis explained, was the amount of time it takes light to travel one centimetre, a meaning he introduced in his research in the 1920s. So next time someone says they'll do something in a *jiffy*, remind them that that gives them precisely 33 trillionths of a second to respond . . .

Livid

originally meant 'bruised'

'The whole thing was a complete disaster! I was livid!' Say something like that in casual conversation today, and you might expect a sympathetic response to the infuriating calamity that has befallen you. Say something like that a few centuries back, and the person you're talking to might start looking to see precisely what part of your body was – well, *livid*.

When it first appeared in the language in the early seventeenth century, *livid* was used to describe anything that was bluish or leaden in colour. So in 1622, Francis Bacon wrote of 'purple . . . livid spots' in a description of an outbreak of sleeping sickness that affected London during the reign of Henry VII. The poet John Gay described sunken 'livid eyes' in a work of 1720. The novelist Ann Radcliffe wrote of 'the livid face' of a corpse in *The Italian* in 1797. Even a seagull's legs can be 'livid' according to an 1828 description of the *Elements of Natural History*.

The word *livid* itself was borrowed into English from French, but has its origins in the Latin word *lividus*, meaning 'bluish'. Colours have long been associated with different emotions, of course, and back in its native Latin, *lividus* could also be used in a figurative sense to mean 'envious', 'malicious' or 'spiteful'. But not one of those is close to the modern use of *livid* to mean 'enraged' or 'infuriated' – so where did that come from?

The association between *lividity* and anger is actually a relatively recent development, and did not begin to appear until the early twentieth century. But this sense of the word – which is said to refer to someone being so angry or affronted that all of the colour drains from their face so that they look bluish or ashen – quickly caught on, and has since all but replaced the original use of *livid* completely.

Except, that is, for one last stronghold. In medicine, *livid* is still used today to mean 'blue-coloured'. Medical documents and diagnoses often refer to bruised, haemorrhaged, or otherwise discoloured skin as *livid*; *lividness* or a *livid* appearance is considered one of the symptoms of cyanosis, a blue coloration of the skin caused by an inadequate amount of oxygen in the blood; and in forensic science, *post-mortem lividity*, or *livor mortis*, is the purplish discoloration of skin seen in dead bodies, caused by blood cells no longer being circulated by the heart pooling in the lower parts of the body under the influence of gravity. The chances of you using that meaning of *livid* in casual conversation are, however, hopefully fairly slim.

Ludicrous

originally meant 'playful'

Remarkably, people have been playing ludo – or at least, versions of ludo – since the sixth century AD. The game first emerged in India, when it was known by the Hindi name *pachisi* (meaning 'twenty-five'), and variations of its gameplay, in which players race to move four counters around a full circle of a board and back to their base, are now found under various names all around the world.

The English name *ludo* literally means 'I play' in Latin, and is a derivative of the verb *ludere*, meaning 'to play', 'to jest' or 'to sport'. *Preludes* and *interludes* both derive from the same root, as do *allusions*, *delusions* and *collusions*. If you're *ludibund* then you're playful or jesting. If you're *ludibrious*, then you're liable to be the butt of the joke. And in the sense of besting or getting the better of someone, the word *elude* also derives from here, as do a handful of rarer words like *ludify* ('to deceive') and *ludificate* ('to mock', 'to frustrate').

Describe something as *ludicrous*, and you're also in the same game-playing ball park. When it first appeared in the early seventeenth century, the adjective *ludicrous* described anything that was sportive or recreational, or else jocular or intended as a joke. Samuel Johnson defined the word *ludicrously* as 'in a manner that may excite laughter' in his dictionary, and by the eighteenth century this meaning had broadened so that *ludicrous* was being used to describe anything frivolous or trifling. Throughout it all, however, the word had largely positive associations – even describing a person as *ludicrous* originally implied that they were quick-witted or could tell a good joke.

But all that was about to change. Thanks to almost two centuries of association with jokes, trivialities and flippancies, by the later 1700s *ludicrous* was beginning to be used to mean 'absurd', 'laughable', 'ridiculous'. Put another way, it had gone from being the joke-teller to the butt of the joke, from the joke itself to the punchline. By the mid nineteenth century, all other uses of the word had fallen away, and *ludicrous* was now only being used in a somewhat negative sense to describe anything or anyone deserving of laughter or derision, and it's this fairly laughable meaning that has remained in place ever since.

Man

originally meant 'person'

In Old English, *man* merely meant 'person' or 'human being', and so applied to both men and women. This gender-neutral meaning might seem odd today, but its influence can still be seen in words like *mankind, manmade, manslaughter, manhandle* and *man-eating,* as well as in somewhat old-fashioned stock phrases like *the fall of man, man or beast* and *man's best friend.*

A few questions remain, though. Firstly, if *man* was once gender-neutral, how did Old English speakers tell men from women (apart from the obvious)? And secondly, when did gender-specific *man* appear, and why?

Well, if you wanted to talk specifically about a *male* person in Old English, you'd have to use the word *wer.* That word too has long since disappeared from the language (although it survives, oddly enough, in the word *werewolf*). *Wer* is also a somewhat distant relative of *virile* (which originally meant 'manly' or 'masculine' before its more sexual connotations emerged in the Middle Ages) and *virtue* (which meant 'manliness', and ultimately 'courage' and 'worthiness', before its meaning settled on 'integrity'). And likewise calling any strong-willed, warrior-like woman a *virago*, essentially means that you're calling her 'mannish'.

The opposite of *wer* in Old English was *wif*, which meant 'woman' (as we discovered under *housewife*). It's from here that the word *wife* is descended, but in Old English *wif* did not necessarily refer to a married woman like it does today. We'll tackle that particular wrinkle when we look at the history of *queen* later. But for now, it's worth pointing out that — just like the *man* of *mankind* and *manmade* — the general sense of *wif* to mean 'woman' still survives in words like *housewife*, *midwife* and even *fish-wife*, which was originally just another word for a female fish-seller before its negative associations with garrulousness and coarseness emerged in the late nineteenth century.

But what about *man*? When did it make the change from gender-neutral to gender-specific? Well, a lot of complicated things happened to *man*, *woman*, *wer* and *wif* in the Middle English period, roughly 800 years ago.

For one, *wif* began to be used much more often to mean

'a married woman'. That left a gap in the language, which the word *woman* eventually filled and has continued to fill ever since. *Woman*, however, literally means 'wife-man' and so contrasts much better with *man* than it does with *wer*. That had the effect of simultaneously pulling *man* closer to *woman*, and thereby ousting the Old English word for 'man', *wer*, from the language. (Are you keeping up?) Despite this change in meaning, however, *man* continued to be used more generally to mean 'any person', but by the end of the thirteenth century it had completely replaced *wer* as the language's go-to word for a specifically male person as well. And it's this meaning that has remained in place ever since. Man alive, that's complicated.

Manage

originally meant 'to control a horse'

So if *man* originally meant 'human', presumably *management* involves *managing* men? You might assume so, but when it first appeared in the language in the mid sixteenth century, *manage* was actually used in a context that had nothing to do with managing men, and everything to do with managing horses:

> The bridegroom . . . had the first course at the quin-
> tain . . . but his mare in his manage did a little so
> titubate, that much ado had his manhood to sit in
> his saddle to escape the foil of a fall: with the help
> of his band yet he recovered himself.

This is an extract (updated into modern English) from a letter written in 1575 by Robert Laneham, a keeper of the privy council chamber under Elizabeth I, after he had attended a wedding party in Kenilworth, Warwickshire. Besides giving us a superb example of the word *titubate* (a sixteenth-century word for a trip or stumble), Laneham's letter shows us precisely what *management* originally entailed.

A *quintain* is an old piece of jousting equipment, comprising a revolving T-shaped frame with a shield or target on one side and a weighed sack on the other. The rider – in this case, the bridegroom himself – would aim to hit the target with his lance, but would have to be careful to dodge the sack as the entire apparatus spun round and tried to knock him out of his saddle. According to Laneham's letter, the bridegroom succeeded in escaping being hit by the bag, but nearly lost his balance as his horse 'titubated' – stumbled or tripped – despite it being 'in his manage'. Wedding parties really just aren't the same these days, are they?

Here, 'in his manage' essentially means 'under his control'. But around the time Laneham was writing this, *manage* had much more specific connotations than it does today, and essentially the earliest sense of the word *manage* in English was 'to handle or train a horse'.

Manage was borrowed into English from Italian in the mid sixteenth century, but its earliest ancestor is the Latin word for 'hand', *manus*. That makes *manage* an etymological cousin of words like *manipulate, manacle, manufacture, manoeuvre* and even *manure* (which, in the sense of cultivating and fertilising land, derives from a French word literally meaning 'to work with the hands').

The Latin word *manus* eventually led to an Italian word *maneggiare*, used to mean 'to handle', 'to use skilfully' and, ultimately, 'to control a horse'. It was the last of these meanings that was borrowed into English first and eventually became our word *manage*. Although the more general use of *manage* to mean 'to control' or 'to administer' was quick to follow, the word maintained its links with horse riding and horse training right through to the late eighteenth century, and this association can still be seen in *manège* – an old word for a riding school, or for horsemanship in general, that was borrowed into English from French in the mid 1600s.

Meerkat

was originally a monkey

In 1801, an English statesman and explorer named Sir John Barrow published an *Account of Travels into the Interior of Southern Africa*. In it, he included the earliest description of one of Africa's most recognisable and most endearing animals:

> Upon those parched plains are also found a great variety of small quadrupeds that burrow in the ground, and which are known to the colonists under the general name of meer-cats . . . [They are] wholly of a bright chestnut colour; the tail shaded with black hairs, bushy, straight, and white at the extremity; ears short and round; on the fore feet five, and the hind feet four, toes; the body and tail each one foot long . . . In general, these animals are easily domesticated.

Leaving Barrow and his pet meerkats aside, now take a look at this description of the fruit of the cashew tree from a travelogue by the Dutch merchant sailor Jan Huygen van Linschoten, written two centuries earlier:

... of form and greatness like a hen's egg, which being ripe is of a gold-yellow colour like a quince, very good and savoury to eat, having a certain sharp taste, and in it a juice that cooleth heat. But because this fruit is not easy to be gathered, as being high trees, the meere-cattes eat them.

    — Jan Huygen van Linschoten, *A Discourse of Voyages into the East and West Indies* (1598)

There are clearly a few inconsistencies here. Barrow's *meerkats* live in holes in the ground in the barren South African plains. Van Linschoten has them eating fruit in the highest, unreachable treetops of the South American rainforest. So what's going on?

The word *meerkat* is thought to have its origins in an old Sanskrit word, *markata*, meaning 'ape'. From there, it was adopted by Dutch sailors and tradesmen working in southeast Asia in the early Middle Ages, and quickly became corrupted: *markata* morphed into *meerkat*, a Dutch word literally meaning 'sea-cat' that was probably initially used as little more than a placeholder name for any four-legged animal found overseas. In this vague sense, *meerkat* was picked up by van Linschoten and many other writers like him and applied to any one of a number of different species of monkey that were discovered during the Age of Exploration. And it was with this meaning that *meerkat* was adopted into English in the late fifteenth century: in its earliest appearance in the language, in a translation of the French folk tale *Reynard the Fox* (1481), the 'mercatte' is listed alongside the marmoset and the baboon as the name of 'a great ape with two great wide eyes'.

Oddly, this original meaning remains in place in modern Dutch, wherein *meerkat* is the name of the guenon, a family of Old World monkeys, while the meerkat itself is called the *stokstaarje*, or 'little stick-tail'. But in Dutch South Africa, at the end of the eighteenth century, a change occurred. There, the name *meerkat* began to be attached not to one of the local species of monkey, but to the small, sociable plains-dwelling mongooses that live across much of the Africa continent, and – in English at least – it is those creatures who have retained the name to this day.

Moment

was originally 90 seconds

Remember a few entries back, when we found out that if someone says they'll only be a *jiffy*, they should really only be 33 trillionths of a second? Well, the next time someone tells you they'll only be a *moment*, you can get your watch at the ready then too — albeit with slightly more time on your hands. That's because a *moment* was originally precisely 90 seconds.

Moment was borrowed into English from French in the late fourteenth century, but its origins can be traced all the way back to the Latin word for 'movement', *momentum*. As a general term for any short amount of time, it probably alludes to the slightest motion or 'movement' of the hands of a clock or the shadow on a sundial, and likewise it was once also used to describe a tiny quantity or weight of something — namely just enough of it to move the gauge on a balance or a set of scales. As well as being used in this somewhat vague sense, however, in medieval timekeeping *moment* also had a much more specific meaning.

The day has been divided into twenty-four hours since antiquity, but before the advent of mechanical clocks in the early Middle Ages, these hours weren't of fixed duration. Historically, the day was taken to start at sunrise and end at sunset, and *vice versa* for night — but *both* day and night were said to comprise twelve hours, no matter how long or short the gap between sunrise and sunset was.

That meant, somewhat confusingly, that during the early medieval period a daytime hour at the height of summer was considerably longer than a night-time hour, and again *vice versa* for night in the depths of winter. Only at the equinox (literally 'equal-night') would all twenty-four hours of the day be precisely equal.

Regardless of how unequal these night-time and day-time hours might be, however, each one was divided in turn into a number of shorter units. Each hour comprised four *points*, of which there were forty-eight during the day and forty-eight during the night. Each *point* was then divided into ten smaller units known as *moments*, of which there were 480 during the day, and 480 during the night. Each *moment* in turn comprised twelve *ounces*, and each ounce contained forty-seven *atoms*. So a *moment*, by medieval reckoning, was ultimately 1/40th of an hour.

Once mechanical clocks began to replace sundials and other less accurate or less reliable timepieces in the early Middle Ages, the old system of dividing the day unequally into two sets of twelve hours between sunrise and sunset became obsolete. The hours of the day were averaged out and standardised as each equalling 1/24th of the day. But although the older system fell out of use, its vocabulary remained.

When the word *moment* first appeared in English in the late 1300s, it was used both as a general term for a short length of time, and as a precise unit of time equal to 1/40th of an hour – or a minute and a half. All the other medieval units also remained in use, each one with newly standardised lengths: a *point* was now fifteen minutes, an *ounce* was 7½ seconds, an atom was 1/376th of a minute, or 0.16 seconds. Over time, however, the use of these definitions slowly dwindled and had disappeared altogether by the late 1600s, so that today only the less specific use of the word *moment* survives.

Myriad

originally meant 10,000

In the third century BC, the Greek scholar Archimedes (he of the bathtub *eureka* moment) wrote a treatise aimed at remedying a shortfall in the Ancient Greek number system. At the time, the Greeks had no means of counting any higher than 10,000 – their number system simply stopped at that point. In order to prove just how inadequate a system that was, Archimedes set about calculating a sum that he knew would lead to an impossibly large solution: namely, the number of grains of sand that it would take to fill the entire universe. Clearly, he had far too much time on his hands.

That being said, Archimedes' *Sand Reckoner*, as it became known, was really not meant to be taken too seriously. Nor was the answer he was searching for meant to be taken as a genuine estimate of such an insanely bizarre query. Instead, he merely used the treatise as a means of outlining and proving the effectiveness of a new number system he had invented that used various compounds of 10,000, one atop the other, to create names for ever higher and higher quantities. And the Greek word for 10,000? That was the original *myriad*.

Etymologists are unsure quite where the word *myriad* actually originated. One theory is that it is somehow related to an ancient word root, *meu–*, that essentially meant 'damp' or 'flowing', and so *myriad* might have alluded to the countlessness or innumerability of the waves or the ocean. Alternatively, it could come from the Greek word for 'ant', *myrmex*, and perhaps originally referred to the enormous numbers of individual ants found in a colony. Whatever its origin, in Ancient Greek a *myriad* – represented by the numeral M – was 10,000, while in Archimedes' number system a *myriad-myriad* was 10^8, or 100,000,000. This number could then be raised to the power of one myriad, $(10^8)^{(10^8)}$, and that figure in turn raised to the power of a *myriad-myriad*, and so on; the highest figure in Archimedes' scale was $((10^8)^{(10^8)})^{(10^8)}$, or, in other words, 1 followed by 80,000,000,000,000,000 (eighty quadrillion) zeros. Considerably larger than 10,000, I think you'll agree.

But as the highest named number in the Greek counting system, the *myriad* was used to mean precisely 10,000, and figuratively any enormous, unspecified amount, much like *umpteen* or *zillion* might be used today. Both of these meanings were then imported into English in the late sixteenth century, but today it is only the vague and unspecified meaning of *myriad* that has survived into modern English.

Only one question remains, then – just how many grains of sand would it take to fill the universe? Well, although he now had the means of counting to $((10^8)^{(10^{\wedge}8)})^{(10^{\wedge}8)}$, Archimedes somewhat underestimated the size of the universe as 10^{14} stadia (roughly two light-years) across, and ultimately calculated that it could be filled with just 10^{63} grains of sand. In fact, the observable universe alone is now known to be 13.8 billion light years across, so Archimedes' calculation was out by a factor of 6.9 billion. Still, at least he had that bathtub thing right.

Nasty

originally meant 'dirty'

There's an old bit of etymological folklore that claims the word *nasty* derives from the name of a nineteenth-century American cartoonist and political caricaturist named Thomas Nast. According to the story, Nast – who is also known for designing the Republican Party's elephant logo – became known for his particularly biting and satirical illustrations of nineteenth-century political figures. Many of his most cutting illustrations were aimed at the corrupt New York statesman William 'Boss' Tweed, whom Nast variously depicted as having a cashbag for a head, as a bloated, corpulent businessman, and as a spoiled and soulless king. Nash's drawings caused Tweed so much consternation ('Stop them damn pictures!' he once exclaimed to one of his aides. 'I don't care what the papers write about me. My constituents can't read. But, damn it, they can see the pictures!') that he reached out to Nash and offered to pay him $100,000 (equivalent to almost $2 million today) to quit his caricaturing and study art in Europe. Nash refused – while Tweed was eventually arrested and jailed for embezzlement.

It's a superb story, but with a problem: Nast's cartoons were at their nastiest in post-Civil War America. The word *nasty* itself, however, is at least seven centuries old.

Nasty first emerged in the language in the late 1300s, when it originally meant 'dirty', 'filthy' or 'befouled'. With Nast out of the picture, the word's true etymology is actually unknown. One theory claims that it might be a clipped form of an Old French word, *villenastre*, meaning 'infamous' or 'notorious'. Another suggests a connection to a Swedish word, *naskig*, meaning 'dirty', or else its Dutch equivalent, *nestig* (literally 'as dirty as a bird's nest'). Connections with *naughty*, an ancient Germanic word *naz*, meaning 'wet' or 'damp', and even an old dialect word *neshy*, meaning 'crumbly' or 'weak' have also been proposed, but none is entirely reliable. Without further written evidence, the word will likely remain a complete mystery.

No matter its origin, however, from its original associations with dirtiness and foulness in the Middle Ages, by the late fifteenth century *nasty* was being used to describe offensive or contemptible people and by the seventeenth century had gained connotations of lewdness or immorality. From there its meaning softened, and in the early 1600s it became more generally associated with vaguely unpleasant or disagreeable things, and in particular anything found offensive to the senses, the meaning by which it is still used today.

But the word had one more trick up its sleeve, which emerged in the early 1800s. Like *mean*, *wicked* and more recently *sick*, in nineteenth-century slang *nasty* began to be used with positive connotations, as a term of approval essentially meaning 'terrific' or 'superb'. As an 1834 edition of New York's *Knickerbocker* magazine explained:

> 'Sling a nasty foot', means to dance exceedingly well. 'She is a nasty looking gal', implies she is a splendid woman. I know not by what singular change this meaning has been given the word nasty, but certain it is, that expressed above, it is considered among the class to which it has reference, as highly complimentary.
>
> — 'Buck Horn Tavern, a Scene in the West',
> *Knickerbocker*, January 1834

Naughty

originally meant 'having nothing'

What is 1 − 1? If you said *zero*, then you've just used a word borrowed from French, that probably has its origins via Latin and Arabic in a Sanskrit word meaning 'empty area of desert'. If you said *nothing*, then you've just used a purely English word that emerged in the middle of the Old English period from a straightforward compound of *none* and *thing*. And if you said *nought*, then you've just used an even older Old English word − formed from a combination of *ne*, a negative-marking adverb, and *aught* − literally meaning 'not anything'. What does all this mean? Well, once upon a time if you had *nought*, then you were literally *naughty*.

When *naughty* first appeared in the language in the early fifteenth century, it meant 'having nothing'. The word could be applied both to tangible possessions as well as intangible ones, so as well as being used to mean 'destitute' or 'needy', *naughty* was also used to describe people with no morals, no empathy, or no sense of decency. Consequently, by the mid 1400s *naughty* was being used in a much stronger sense than it is today to mean 'wicked', 'depraved' or, in relation to animals, 'vicious' or 'untamed'. This sense of immorality or savagery continued to strengthen throughout the Middle

Ages, so that by the sixteenth century *naughty* was being used to mean 'licentious' or 'sexually provocative': in Tudor slang, a *naughty pack* was a notoriously promiscuous person, while when the Earl of Gloucester calls Regan a 'naughty lady' in Act III of Shakespeare's *King Lear*, he's calling her a lot worse than 'misbehaved'.

Throughout the sixteenth and seventeenth centuries, *naughty* continued to be used in a number of negative senses, many of which have long since disappeared from the language. At various times in its history, *naughty* has been used to mean everything from 'harmful' and 'unfavourable' to 'unhealthy', 'inappropriate', 'unwholesome' and even 'foul-smelling'. Someone described as *naughty-tongued* would be a habitual user of foul or blasphemous language. One sixteenth-century herbalist outlined a cure for 'naughty ulcers', in which *naughty* is used to mean 'severe' or 'chronic'. And elsewhere in *King Lear*, Shakespeare even went on to label bad weather as 'naughty', calling a stormy night 'a naughty night to swim in'.

Having reached peak *naughtiness* in the sixteenth century, however, the word has since weakened and today is seldom used except to mean 'misbehaved' or 'mischievous'. This sense first emerged in the early 1600s, and, as all other meanings have steadily fallen out of use, has since established itself as the word's most familiar meaning. In more recent decades, however, its long-lost inappropriateness has re-emerged.

Despite its decidedly modern feel, the term *naughty nineties* originally referred to the comparative loosening of Victorian-era morals that occurred in the 1890s and was first used in 1925. According to the *Oxford English Dictionary* the colloquialism *naughty bits* was first used in a *Monty Python* sketch in 1972. And as for *naughty but nice*, it originated in the lyrics of an old English music-hall song written in 1871:

Of love at first sight you have heard. Well, I'm a
    luckless cove,
And love a lass upon my soul who lives in
    Westbourne Grove.
At the charming game of croquet I have been her
    partner twice,
I love her, ain't it naughty — well, it's naughty, but
    it's nice.

— Arthur Lloyd,
It's Naughty, but it's Nice (1871)

Nephew

originally meant 'grandson'

No one is entirely sure why we say 'Bob's your uncle!', but the most widely held theory is that the Bob in question is nineteenth-century Conservative Prime Minister Robert Cecil, whose appointment of his nephew (and future fellow Prime Minister) Arthur Balfour as Chief Secretary of Ireland in 1887 was as unexpected as it was unpopular. It was widely claimed that Balfour had secured the position for no reason other than the fact that his uncle was the Prime Minister, and ultimately 'Bob's your uncle!' came to be used of any outcome achieved a lot more easily that might have been imagined.

But Robert Cecil's flagrant nepotism has a lot more to do with Balfour being his *nephew* than it might first appear. The word *nepotism* itself actually derives from the Latin word for a nephew, *nepos*, as do a handful of obscure but eminently useful words like *nepotation* (meaning 'reckless, self-indulgent behaviour') and *nepotious* (an adjective describing someone who is extremely fond of their nephew or niece). Another word from the murkier corners of the dictionary, however, points us in a different direction altogether: *pronepote* was a sixteenth-century dialect word for a great-grandson.

The original meaning of *nepos* in Latin was 'grandson', while the secondary meaning of 'nephew' emerged much later, around the fourth century AD. Both these meanings then co-existed for centuries to come: Latin *nepos* gave way to the French *neveu*, which was adopted into English in the early fourteenth century and became *nephew*. Originally, it was used as a byword for both the son of one's brother or sister, and for a grandson, or more broadly, a male descendant.

Over the years, *nephew* picked up a number of other meanings and connotations, including 'a distant relative found on a line of succession' in the late fourteenth century, and even 'the illegitimate son of a pope or cleric' in the late sixteenth century. By the late 1700s, however, most of these alternative meanings had disappeared – as had the older use of *nephew* to mean 'grandson'. By the turn of the eighteenth-nineteenth centuries the word's current meaning was the only one still standing.

But why did the word have two seemingly incompatible meanings for so long anyway? It's a good question, to which the answer is not immediately clear. But one theory is that it is all to do with the medieval rules of succession.

Imagine a father, wishing to pass on his title or his estate to his offspring, dies either childless or – perish the thought! – with only daughters and no male heir. According to the uncompromising rules of primogeniture, his daughters would not even get a look in on their father's estate, and instead the whole kit and caboodle would be passed on to his closest male descendant, which in many cases would be either his eldest grandson, or else the eldest son of his brother or sister. In that way, *nephew* acted as a catch-all term essentially meaning 'any male descendant that isn't one's immediate son', and it is that impreciseness that allowed both meanings of the word to survive in the language for so long. Eventually, as these somewhat old-fashioned rules began to be challenged and abandoned, the meaning standardised and Bob's your uncle – we were left with the *nephews*, and the *nepotism*, we have today.

Nice

originally meant 'ignorant'

Let's be honest, as compliments go *nice* is a fairly bland one. But at least it has positive connotations – a *nice* person is pleasant, agreeable and even-tempered. The kind of person who is only too happy to help, only too happy to be happy. But things haven't always been quite so nice.

When it first emerged in the language in the Middle English period, *nice* was used to mean almost anything but pleasant and even-tempered. The word itself derives from the Latin *nescius*, meaning 'ignorant' (or rather 'not knowing', the *–scius* part being derived from the same root as words like *science*, *prescience* and *conscience*) and that empty-headedness was carried through into English in the early 1300s. At that point, *nice* was essentially used to mean 'foolish' or 'simple-minded', although in its early days it could also be used as a noun, as another word for a fool or blockhead. By the end of the fourteenth century, however, things had started to change.

Nice went on to gain connotations of lustfulness and wantonness. A *nice* person could now just as easily be a scandalous libertine as an empty-headed nincompoop, and that was just the beginning. Over the centuries that followed, *nice* came to be used with a dizzying array of meanings and in an equally dizzying array of contexts.

By the turn of the fifteenth century, it had picked up connotations of extravagance and ostentatiousness, cowardice and unmanliness, shyness, timidity and unwillingness, sloth and sluggishness. By the sixteenth century, it was being used to mean everything from 'fragile' and 'insubstantial' to 'meticulous' and 'fussy', by way of 'trivial', 'hard to please', 'sensitive' and even 'not easily understood'. By the seventeenth century, it had come to mean 'pampered', 'cultured' and 'acutely aware'. By the eighteenth century, it meant 'precise' or 'exacting' – and it was then that the word's positive connotations finally started to appear. Soon *nice* was being used to mean 'satisfactory', 'attractive', 'respectable' and eventually 'agreeable', 'pleasant' and 'good-natured', the meaning by which it tends to be used today. *Nice* had, quite clearly, been on quite a nice journey.

But why? Why should such an unassuming word have taken such an extraordinary route through the language, taking in just about every positive and negative quality along the way? Why should, for instance, the 'nice wenches' mentioned in Shakespeare's *Love's Labour's Lost* be dishonourable, dissolute women, while the 'nice fashion' in *Henry V* be another word for fussy, overly particular behaviour? No one, admittedly, is entirely sure.

Glancing back through all the long-lost meanings of *nice*, it's at least possible to chart a path from negative attributes – ignorance, cowardliness, dissolution – to more neutral attributes – shyness, triviality, meticulousness – and finally more positive connotations – attractiveness, pleasantness, an easy-going nature. But quite what sparked these changes, and the overall change from positive to negative, is unclear. It's just a nice story.

Noon

originally meant 3pm

Nowadays, with our electric lights and alarm clocks, our new day begins at midnight. But to the Romans, forced to confine their working day to the hours of daylight, the day began at sunrise. The Roman day was nevertheless still divided into twenty-four hours, and it's from the *nona hora* or 'ninth hour' of the Roman day that we have ended up with the word *noon*.

As etymological stories go, that's a fairly straightforward one, or at least it would be, were it not for one small problem. Because the Roman day began at sunrise, its timing was seasonal, so your working day would begin at a different time in, say, March, than it would in August. Not only that, but (as was the case with *moment*) both day and night were always taken as comprising twelve hours each, and so, due to the fluctuating start of the day, an hour in summer was roughly seventy-five minutes long while an hour in the winter was closer to forty-five minutes. In response to this inconsistency (as was also the case with *moment*) a standardised method of timekeeping eventually emerged, based on the equal length of day and night at the equinox. So, by the medieval period, the day was taken to start at a time roughly corresponding to what we would now call six o'clock in the morning – which ultimately made the ninth hour of the day three o'clock in the afternoon.

What all this means is that when the word *noon* first emerged in the English language in the early Old English period, it wasn't another name for midday but 3pm – as in this extract (translated into modern English) from a ninth-century medical textbook:

> Take a bramble apple, and lupins . . . pound them then sift them . . . put the dust into milk, drip thrice some holy water upon them, administer this to drink at three hours, at undern [*at 9am*], at midday, and at noon.
> — *Bald's Leechbook* (*c.* 9th century)

This definition was further reinforced by the traditions of the early Christian church, whose day was divided into eight liturgical hours or 'offices' – *matins, lauds, prime, terce, sext, none, vespers, compline* – corresponding to the Roman clock. So *prime* was an early morning prayer corresponding to the first hour of the Roman day, or roughly 6am; *sext* was a midday prayer, recited at the sixth hour of the day; and *none*, like *noon*, was a mid-afternoon prayer recited at the ninth hour of day, or 3pm.

All that began to change sometime around the turn of the thirteenth century, when *noon* began to be used as another name for midday – although no one is quite sure why. It could be that the liturgical prayers associated with 3pm were moved to midday, and simply took the word *noon* with them. Or it could be that the timing of the main meal of the day was moved from later in the afternoon to twelve o'clock. Or there could be a cultural shift in action, sparked by the Norman Conquest, that saw the working day start earlier than it ever had before, thereby altering all the names associated with the different times of day. Or, of course, it could be a combination of all or some of these explanations. But whatever the reason, by the early sixteenth century the use of *noon* to mean three o'clock in the afternoon had all but vanished, leaving us with the midday meaning we still use today.

Oaf

originally meant 'elf'

Should you ever be unlucky enough to encounter one, calling someone an *oaf* – or else picking someone up for their *oafish* behaviour – nowadays means that they're foolish, doltish, or unsophisticated and uncouth. An *oaf* is a dunderhead. A blockhead. A noddypoll, if you want to drop a little sixteenth-century insult into the mix. But that meaning is actually a relatively recent development that first emerged in the language in the early 1700s. A century before then, *oaf* was used in a much more unusual and unexpected way — as another name for an impish hobgoblin.

Oaf is derived from the Old English word for an elf, *ælf*, which in turn was probably borrowed into English from Scandinavia. *Oaf* — or *ouphe* as it was usually spelled back then — retained this supernatural meaning when it first began to be used in the language in the early 1600s:

> Nan Page my daughter, and my little son,
> And three or four more of their growth we'll dress
> Like urchins, oafs, and fairies, green and white,
> With rounds of waxen tapes on their heads,
> And rattles in their hands.
>
> — William Shakespeare,
> *The Merry Wives of Windsor* (c. 1602)

Besides being used as just another name for an imp or goblin, however, there was more to the oaf's story than Shakespeare makes evident here. According to folklore, an *oaf* was originally a changeling, the child of an elf or fairy who was swapped with a human infant to be raised by a human mother:

> Oaf . . . a foolish child left by malevolent ouphs or fairies, in the place of one more witty, which they

steal away . . . A changeling, a foolish child left by the fairies.

> — Samuel Johnson, *A Dictionary of*
> *the English Language* (1755)

According to some traditional accounts, legends like this one derive from the old belief that the children of elves and fairies could only be raised on human breast milk, and so needed to be swapped with human babies in order to survive. Others claim that the elves would be liable to snatch any child who had not been baptised, and so raising the child within the church was the only way to protect them. And others claimed the elves gave the human children to the Devil, to stop him from stealing their own offspring. Whatever the original legend might have been, it was this association between oafs and changelings – the malformed, illegitimate offspring of imps and monsters – that eventually led to the word's association with stupidity and foolishness. Eventually, as the superstitious beliefs of old folklore began to be abandoned, this meaning replaced the supernatural one, and remains the only meaning of the word still in use today.

Obnoxious

originally meant 'exposing to harm'

Obstacle. Obstruction. Obstinate. Obnoxious. What is it about *ob—* words that makes so many of them so *objectionable?* The answer lies in the meaning of the prefix *ob—* itself.

Ob began life as a Latin word, one of the many meanings of which was some sense of moving or acting against something, or of concealing or blocking it. It is from here that a number of *ob—* words gained their associations with barriers and hindrances (as in *obstacle* and *obstruction*), denseness or dull-wittedness (as in *obtuse* and *obscure*), suppression and disguise (as in *obfuscate* and *oblique*), and stubbornness and pig-headedness (as in *obdurate* and *obstinate*). Hence *obloquy* is contradictory, opposing speech. To *obumbrate* something is to cast a shadow over it. To *obambulate* is to walk around it. And even somewhat neutral *ob—* words can trace their roots back to here, as an *obstetrician* is literally someone who stands in front of an expectant mother, while describing something as *obvious* literally means that it's very visibly blocking your path.

But *obnoxious* is slightly different. It bears another distinct sense of *ob*, namely a 'movement towards' something rather than against or in front of it. But if that's the case, how did *obnoxious* end up being such an obnoxious word?

At the root of *obnoxious* (as well as *noxious, nuisance* and *innocuous*) is the Latin word *nocere*, meaning 'to harm' or 'to injure'. *Innocuous* ultimately means 'not harmful' (the opposite of which is *nocuous*), while *nuisance* is literally damage or injury, and something that is *noxious* is literally harmful or detrimental. If something is *obnoxious*, ultimately, then it quite literally puts you in harm, moves you towards something or somewhere harmful, or exposes you to danger. And in that sense, it's probably the worst *ob–* word we've got.

Obnoxious maintained this sense of 'exposure to harm' when it first appeared in the language in the mid 1500s. Other meanings were quick to emerge however, so that by the end of the sixteenth century *obnoxious* was also being used to mean 'answerable' or 'subject to another's power or authority', in the sense of someone being liable for the damage or injury caused to someone else. By the seventeenth century this meaning had broadened again, so that *obnoxious* was now being used to mean 'punishable', or essentially 'deserving of harm or injury', and ultimately 'potentially hurtful' or 'potentially injurious'. And from there, it was merely a short sidestep to the more familiar modern meaning of 'unpleasant', or 'disagreeable', which first emerged in the mid 1600s.

Obsess

originally meant 'torment'

Another *ob–* word with somewhat unpleasant origins is *obsess*. Far removed from its current meaning, when it first appeared in the language back in the mid 1400s it essentially meant 'to torment' or 'to haunt'. But it was often also used much more specifically in relation to evil spirits, which were once upon a time believed to be able to control or 'obsess' a person's body:

> A man is said to be obsest when an evill spirit foll-weth him, troubling him at divers times and seeking opportunity to enter into him.
> — John Bullokar, *An English Expositor, or Compleat Dictionary . . . of the Hardest Words* (1616)

The word *obsess* itself is a derivative of the Latin verb *obsidere*. It literally meant 'to sit opposite to', but was often used in a more figurative sense to mean 'to watch over closely' or 'occupy', particularly with connotations of acting oppressively or against someone's will. A derivative verb, *obdure*, emerged in English in the late 1600s meaning 'to beset', or 'to encompass entirely', while *obsess* itself was also used to mean 'to besiege' in the late sixteenth century. The association between *obsess* and evil spirits, however, alludes to the notion of some malevolent force entering a person's body from the outside, much like an invading army might *obdure* or impose themselves on a besieged fortress or city. In that sense, a ghostly *obsession* was different from a ghostly *possession*, in which the supernatural forces involved somehow emerged from within a person's body, rather than being imposed on them by external means.

By the mid sixteenth century, this paranormal meaning of *obsess* had begun to broaden, so that the word was being used in a weaker sense to mean simply 'to harass' or 'to beleaguer'. By the mid nineteenth century, this meaning had broadened again, so that *obsess* was being used to mean 'to preoccupy someone's mind', or 'to give cause for concern'. And eventually, more than 200 years after it first appeared in the language, to be *obsessed* no longer meant 'to be malevolently possessed' and instead had come to mean 'to be extremely worried or preoccupied about something', the sense that still survives today.

Ostracism

When it comes to showing someone how much you dislike
them, the English language has an array of words and phrases
to account for your actions. People have been *giving the cold
shoulder* to their unwanted companions since the early 1800s:
the phrase was first used by Sir Walter Scott – and may in
fact be his own invention – perhaps based on the notion of
giving an unwanted house guest a cheap 'cold shoulder' of
mutton so that they don't outstay their welcome. Unpopular
people have been *sent to Coventry* since the mid eighteenth
century at least, perhaps in allusion to some royalist soldiers
banished to the town by Oliver Cromwell and shunned by its
parliamentary inhabitants during the English Civil War. And
people have been *ostracised* from society even longer: *ostracism*
has its origins way back in Ancient Greece, when far from
being a byword for merely shunning or cold-shouldering
someone, *ostracism* was a democratic process with an extraordinarily uncompromising outcome.

Back in Ancient Athens, a procedure was held each year
in which the city's populace could elect to have someone
they disliked banished from the city for a total of ten years.

A special stall – effectively a polling station – would be erected in the local marketplace where everyone in the city who was eligible to vote could go and give the name of someone they wanted rid of. The name in question would be written on an *ostrakon* (a potsherd or broken shard of pottery, the Ancient Greek equivalent of scrap paper) and dropped into an urn. At the end of the voting period, the names would be counted up and anyone whose name appeared at least 6,000 times, or anyone who received the most votes so long as a total of 6,000 votes had been cast in total, would be given ten days to leave the city, no questions asked. The banishment lasted anything up to a decade, and anyone caught returning to the city would be immediately executed.

It might all sound impossibly harsh, but there was a core of rational thinking behind this original Athenian *ostracism*. Far from merely being a means of ejecting some unpopular public figure from society, ostracism was seen more as a method of maintaining political harmony. More often than not, those who ended up being expelled from the city were ambitious, ruthless officials and politicians whose increasingly power-hungry actions threatened to unbalance the city's politics. In that way, Athenian ostracism was often pre-emptive, stopping potential future tyrants from gaining too much sway before it was too late and giving them a much needed reminder of the power both of democracy and of those whom they were actually in public office to serve.

Moreover, ostracism alone was seen as punishment enough – the expelled party was not imprisoned, lost none of their money or property, and at the end of their banishment was permitted to return to the city, should they so desire, without dishonour. There are even records of ostracisms being repealed: when Cimon, a noted Greek statesman and military strategist, advocated providing military aid to Sparta during a series of uprisings in southern Greece, he was branded a revolutionist and ostracised from Athens in 461 BC. But after several years in exile, he was permitted to return to the city to help broker a peace treaty between the two states.

It was this Ancient Greek meaning of *ostracism* that was imported into the English language in the late sixteenth century. The word quickly caught on and by the early 1600s was being used as merely a general term for banishment or exclusion from society, and it's in this more figurative sense that the word survives today. Regrettably, the actual practice of political *ostracism* never quite caught on in the same way.

Palaver

originally meant 'a conversation in different languages'

When European traders first began working their way down the coast of Africa in the late Middle Ages, they soon hit upon a problem. In order to trade with the local peoples, they first had to work out a means of conversing with people who had little, if any, knowledge of their culture and language – and *vice versa*. No doubt after much effort and mutual cooperation, a middle ground was eventually established, and as pidgin languages combining elements of both European and local African languages began to emerge, trade between Europe and Africa finally began to flourish.

To Portuguese traders especially, dealing with their colonies in Cape Verde and Guinea, these trade negotiations and disputes became known as *palavras*, a Portuguese word literally meaning 'words' or 'talks' (and which can trace its history all the way back to the Latin for 'parable', *parabola*). *Palavra* was in turn then borrowed into the local African vernacular as *palaver*, where it came to be used to mean 'discussion' or 'conference'. And from there, towards the end of the seventeenth century, it was finally passed back to the English traders and explorers who started joining their continental counterparts in expanding trade in Africa.

It was in the sense of a quarrel or dispute – and in particular one concerning a trade negotiation, or one held between two or more people speaking different languages – that the word *palaver* first appeared in English in the early 1700s. A handful of secondary meanings, including 'coaxing, persuasive chatter' and 'pointless talk or idle gossip', were quick to follow, before the more familiar use of *palaver* as another word for a fuss or a tiresome, long drawn-out rigmarole – often over some ultimately trivial matter – finally emerged in British English in the late nineteenth century; the word's American sense of 'jargon' or 'gobbledygook' followed in the early 1900s.

We might have taken the word *palaver* from West Africa, but that's not to say that it ceased to be used there too:

We now resumed our journey, and about eleven o'clock reached a walled town called Tambacunda [*in Senegal*] where we were well received. Here we remained four days, on account of a palaver which was held on the following occasion: [*a man named*] Modi Lemina . . . had formerly married a woman of this town who had borne him two children; he afterwards went to Manding [*in Mali*] and remained there eight years, without sending any account to his deserted wife; who seeing no prospect of his return, at the end of three years had married another man . . . After all the circumstances had been

fully investigated in an assembly of the chief men, it
was determined that the wife should make her choice,
and be at liberty either to return to the first husband,
or continue with the second.

   – Mungo Park, *Travels in the Interior of Africa* (1799)

To this day, the word *palaver* remains in use in a number
of African countries and languages in its original sense of
a conference or discussion, typically over some manner of
dispute or moral disagreement, as in this scandalous affair
recorded by the Scottish explorer Mungo Park. 'She found
it a difficult matter to make up her mind and requested
time for consideration,' Park continued, 'but I think I could
perceive that first love would carry the day.'

Passenger

originally meant 'pilot'

The origins of the word *passenger* are French: the verb *passer*,
meaning 'to go by', gave way to an Old French adjective *passagier*,
meaning 'travelling' or 'itinerant', and that in turn eventually
began to be used as a noun meaning 'someone who travels'.

That might sound vaguely similar to how we use the word *passenger* today, but when *passenger* first began to appear in English texts and documents in the fourteenth century, things were different. Back then, *passenger* was used in an array of different senses and contexts (no one is entirely decided which was the first to emerge) almost all of which were entirely at odds with the word's meaning as it is today.

Far from being a word for a paying fare or customer, for instance, one of the earliest recorded meanings of *passenger* was as another word for the captain or operator of a ferry, or for the keeper of a fording point of a river. In this context — unearthed as far back as 1346, as the job title of a Norfolk man named Johannes de Heuingham — the original *passenger* was not a passenger himself, but rather a crew member or an official responsible for conveying other people around.

Nor, for that matter, was it only the captain of the ferry who could be the passenger, but the ferry itself. Records of ships called *passajours* have been found in Middle English documents dating back to the 1330s, while a letter written by the English landowner Sir John Paston in 1473 recalls how 'two passagerys off Dovre were takyn'.

And nor did the original *passenger* have to have anything at all to do with any kind of transport: back in the mid 1300s, a *passenger* could just as easily have been a pedestrian or a passer-by, or someone travelling from one place to another on foot:

> A pilgrim or passenger that cometh from foreign coun-
> tries rejoiceth when he restoreth to his resting place,
> where he hopes in peace and quiet to abide.
>
> — John Lydgate, *The Pilgrimage of*
> *the Life of Man* (*c.* 1430)

Eventually all these older meanings of *passenger* began to fall out of use. As a name for a ford-keeper or ferry captain, *passenger* survived until the late sixteenth century (when it was defined in a 1574 *Dictionary of English, Latin and French* as 'one that conveyeth over many'). As another name for the ferry itself, it remained in use until the early seventeenth century. And as another word for a passer-by or pedestrian, it survived right through to the early eighteenth century (although it remains in use in a handful of regional dialects, most notably Scots). As all these uses dwindled, the modern meaning of *passenger* – defined by the *Oxford English Dictionary* as, 'a person in or on a conveyance other than its driver, pilot, or crew' – took their place, having first appeared in the language in the early 1500s, and it is this meaning that has remained in use ever since.

Pedagogue
was originally a slave

Teachers have been known as *teachers* since the mid thirteenth century. Before then, *master* was probably the most widely used term for those in the teaching profession in the Old English period, but around that time there was also a whole host of inventive and somewhat euphemistic titles for teachers, including *cilda-herde* (which literally means 'child-herder') and *láreów* (a fairly uncompromising term that literally means 'knowledge slave'). But, oddly, that isn't the only connection we have between teaching and servitude.

The word *pedagogue* first appeared in English as another name for a teacher or instructor in the late 1300s, but its origins stretch back considerably further than that. Although borrowed into English from French, the French in turn took the word from Latin, while it was the Latin-speaking Romans who had adopted the word from Ancient Greece. At its very earliest, the word combines the Greek words for 'child', *pais*, and 'guide' or 'leader', *agogos*, and originally referred to a slave who would be given responsibility for accompanying or escorting a child to school.

How long the word maintained this association with slavery is unclear, but by the time *pedagogue* began to appear in

Latin texts its use as another word for a teacher was already beginning to gain ground, and it seems clear that all links to servitude had long disappeared by the time the word was picked up by French (and ultimately English) in the medieval period. Elsewhere in Europe, however, a different etymological branch was starting to develop.

Around the same time that *pedagogue* was adopted from Latin and into French, it also found its way into Italian where – perhaps under some kind of influence from an identical word for a foot soldier, or else some inflected form of the original Latin word – it steadily transformed into *pedante*. By the mid fifteenth century, *pedante* was the standard Italian word for a schoolteacher or tutor, and it was in this sense that the word *pedant* was borrowed into English in the late 1500s.

But while *pedagogue* has shaken off its negative associations with slavery and servitude, *pedant* went the opposite way: before long, it had picked up all kinds of negative implications and was being used with connotations of arrogance, boastfulness and nit-picking sophistry. By the turn of the sixteenth century, *pedant* was being used to refer to someone who proudly flaunts their intelligence or knowledge over others, or who reveres learning and academic ability over all else, and ultimately came to be used of someone who steadfastly adheres to strict rules, or quibbles over the slightest and most trifling of details or instructions. Put another way, from *pedants* to *pedagogues,* etymology has not been too kind to the teaching profession.

℘encil

originally meant 'paintbrush'

It is easy to presume that as names of two similar items of stationery, both *pen* and *pencil* are etymologically related, but in fact they are entirely unconnected. *Pen* was borrowed into English from French in the early fourteenth century and derives from the Latin word *penna,* meaning 'feather' – a reference to the quill feathers once widely used as writing implements. That makes *pen* an etymological cousin of words such as *pennant* (the name of a type of tapering flag), *empennage* (the word for the arrangement of flat, broad fins on the tail of an aircraft that provide stability) and even *penne* pasta (which is named for its similarity to the hollow point at the bottom of a quill). *Pencil,* on the other hand, is a derivative of the Latin word *peniculus,* which means that its etymological cousins are somewhat less romantic: the likes of *penicillin, penicillium* bacteria and *penis.* (No, really.)

Penis actually meant 'tail' in Latin, and that made a *peniculus* literally a 'little tail'. But our word *pencil* did not emerge directly from there: picture the tail of a creature like a lion, with a thick tuft or ball of fur at the end of it, and you'll be along the right lines of what happened next.

> Pencil. n. . . . I. A small brush of hair which painters dip in their colours.
> To Pencil. v. [from the noun] To paint.
>
> – Samuel Johnson,
> *A Dictionary of the English Language* (1755)

Yes, thanks to its association with Latin *penises* and lions' tufty tails, a *pencil* was originally a paintbrush. In fact, that meaning is a lot older than Johnson's definition might suggest: Geoffrey Chaucer figuratively refers to 'painting' a story with a 'subtle pencil' in his *Canterbury Tales* (*c.* 1387), while the *Oxford English Dictionary* has unearthed a reference to an artist's 'pinsel' as far back as the mid 1320s.

Pencils as we know them today, however, first began to emerge in the late sixteenth century, so that by the time Samuel Johnson compiled his dictionary in the mid 1700s, he had to include both meanings of the word – beneath the definition quoted above, he included this:

> 2. A black lead pen, with which cut to a point they write without ink.

But that's not to say that the earlier use of *pencil* to mean 'paintbrush' has disappeared from the language altogether: fine artists' paintbrushes are still sometimes known as *pencils* or *pencil-brushes* today, while in zoological and botanical contexts the word is sometimes even used to refer to a small bristly tuft of hairs or fibres, just like those you can see at the end of a lion's tail. Just make sure that it's the tail you're looking at.

Penguin

was originally an auk

In August 1577, Sir Francis Drake's *Golden Hind* arrived in the Southern Ocean and began rounding the Magellan Strait heading for the Pacific. On 20 August, the ship's admiral Francis Fletcher recorded in the ship's logbook:

In these Islands we found great reliefe and plenty of good victualls, for infinite were the number of fowle, which the Welsh men named Pengwin . . . [They] breed and lodge at land, and in the day tyme goe downe to the sea to feed, being soe fatt that they can but goe, and their skins cannot be taken from their bodyes without tearing off the flesh, because of their exceeding fatnes.

Fletcher's account provides us with the earliest description of a penguin we know of — but then again, there's this:

> New found land is in a temperate Climate . . . There are Sea Guls, Murres [*guillemots*], Duckes, wild Geese, and many other kinds of birdes store, too long to write, especially at one Island named Penguin, where wee may driue them on a planke into our ship as many as shall lade her. These birdes are also called Penguins, and cannot flie.

If you know your natural history, something here might seem a little odd: penguins are found only in the Southern Hemisphere, so what are they doing in Newfoundland off the North American coast?

That second quote isn't from Drake's *Golden Hind* logbook, but rather a letter written in November 1578 by a Bristol merchant sailor named Anthony Pankhurst to the renowned English geographer Richard Hakluyt. The penguins Parkhurst is talking about though aren't the same penguins we know today — in fact, the penguins he's talking about haven't been seen by anybody for 150 years.

Parkhurst is actually describing the great auk — a tall,

flightless, black-and-white seabird once native to much of the North Atlantic. Although it has now long been hunted to extinction (the last known breeding pair were killed by fishermen off the coast of Iceland in 1844), in Drake and Fletcher's day they were still widely abundant – so abundant that they could apparently be driven in huge numbers from 'Penguin Island', along a plank, and onto a ship to provide food for the crew.

Fletcher's quote might predate Parkhurst's by a little over a year, but it's thought that the birds Parkhurst wrote about were the original 'penguins' – after all, for there to be a place called 'Penguin Island' in 1578, we can presume the word *penguin* was in use in reference to the great auk long before then. Drake's crew, meanwhile, would have presumably been familiar with the sea birds they knew from back home, and so when they saw remarkably similar flightless black-and-white birds in the freezing cold waters of the Southern Ocean, they either mistook them for the auks they knew from home, or else simply referred to them by the same name, *penguin*, because they looked so similar.

The word *penguin* itself is something of a mystery. One theory claims that it might be related to a Latin word, *pinguis*, meaning 'plump' or 'fatty', but a more likely explanation rests with the Welshmen in Fletcher's crew: *penguin* likely derives from the Welsh *pen gwyn*, or 'white head', a reference to a bright white patch of plumage that the great auk had between its bill and eyes. Either way, it is clear that the original *penguins* were not only from the Atlantic rather than the Antarctic, but they weren't even penguins at all.

𝒫eripatetic

was originally a follower of Socrates

Today you're most likely to come across the word *peripatetic* in reference to employment, and in particular with itinerant or specialised professionals (most notably teachers) who are not attached to any particular institution and so are free to move from place to place as required. Originally, however, *peripatetic* was a noun: spelled with a capital P, a *Peripatetic* was a follower or advocate of the Ancient Greek philosopher Aristotle, and it was in this sense that the word made its debut appearance in English in the mid fifteenth century. But how are those two meanings connected?

Etymologically, *peripatetic* brings together two Ancient Greek roots: *peri*, meaning 'around' or 'about' (as in *perimeter* and *periphery*), and *pateo*, a Greek verb meaning 'walk', 'tread' or 'trample' (and which is a distant relative of *path*). Hence *peripatetic* literally means 'walking around' – while to *peripateticate* is to 'walk about' and *peripateticism* is the act of travelling or wandering around on foot. And if there's one thing Aristotle enjoyed more than anything else, it was a bit of peripateticism.

At the Lyceum, the Athenian sports ground/scholarly gymnasium he used as a venue for debating and teaching, Aristotle was known for his habit of wandering, seemingly aimlessly, around the corridors and gardens while he delivered his lessons and debated with his students. This was a habit he apparently picked up from his own mentor, Plato, who had a walkway called a *peripatos* specifically set aside at his school, the Academy, to do precisely that. The custom earned Aristotle and his followers the nickname *Peripatetikos* (literally 'given to walking about'), and so when the word *Peripatetic*-with-a-capital-P first appeared in English in the mid 1400s, it referred exclusively to Aristotelian beliefs and techniques.

Later writers commandeered this originally philosophical term for their own needs, and began employing it in a host of more figurative contexts. By the early 1600s, it was being used to refer to someone who likes to wander aimlessly, or likes to travel around. In 1607, the Elizabethan playwright Thomas Tomkins referred to sleepwalking as 'the peripatetic disease'. Galleries and corridors suitable for walking in were labelled *peripatetic* in the mid seventeenth century. Charles Dickens described a rambling, long-winded speech as 'peripatetic' in *Our Mutual Friend* (1865). And in the 1800s, the word was finally attached to itinerant teachers or teaching, not specifically associated with any particular school. Understandably the Aristotelian use of the word *peripatetic* still remains in use in philosophic contexts today, but it is these broader uses of the word that have now long since become the word's most familiar meaning.

Pink

originally meant 'dark yellow'

Look up *pink* in a dictionary, and you might be surprised to find just how diverse a word it actually is. As well as being the name of a colour midway between red and white, *pink* is the common name of a family of flowers in the genus *Dianthus*, as well as a regional nickname for the corn-cockle and cuckoo-flower plants. It's also the name of a small flat-bottomed sailing vessel, and an old nickname for a minnow, a young salmon and a chaffinch. A *pink* can be a decorative hole or eyelet on a garment, as well as a puncture wound or a hole made by a knife or dagger. As a verb it can be used to mean 'to perforate' or 'to puncture a hole', as well as 'to give an ornate trim to a garment', 'to peer slyly or suspiciously', 'to drip or trickle' and 'to apply rouge to the face'. As an adjective it can be used to describe eyes that are small in size or half closed (*pink-eye*, long before it became a common name for conjunctivitis, meant 'a partly closed eye'). And, derived from the Pinkerton detective agency established in Chicago in 1855, a *pink* can even be a nickname for a private investigator. Of all these definitions, however, the use of *pink* as the name of a colour was the first to emerge – but that's not to say that *pink* has always been pink.

According to the *Oxford English Dictionary*, back in the mid fifteenth century *pink* was originally the name of 'a yellowish or greenish-yellow lake pigment made by combining a vegetable colouring matter with a white base', with varieties known as *English pink*, *Dutch pink*, *Italian pink* and even *brown pink*. In other words, *pink* was originally yellow. So how exactly did this colour change come about?

Actually, the two colourful meanings of *pink* – namely murky yellow and pale red – are etymologically unrelated. No one is entirely sure how the yellow form of *pink* earned its name, although one highly convincing theory claims that it might derive, for obvious reasons, from an old German word *pinkeln*, literally meaning 'to piss'. This yellowish sense of *pink* actually remains in use today (albeit fairly infrequently) in artistic contexts, but it is the pale red version of *pink* that is by far the more familiar meaning.

That kind of *pink* takes its name from those *Dianthus* flowers or 'pinks' mentioned earlier. Various different species of *Dianthus* have been known as *pinks* since the mid 1500s, the name unsurprisingly referring to the flowers' bright magenta petals. According to legend, these flowers were a personal favourite of Elizabeth I and so were grown and sold all across England during the late Tudor period. And, as a result, bright pink pinks became not only extremely popular but extremely familiar, helping once and for all to attach the name *pink* to a pale red rather than murky yellow colour.

Potpourri

was originally a stew

Ah, there's really nothing better to freshen up a room than a fragrant bowl of *potpourri*:

> Pot pourri . . . a Spanish dish of many several meats boiled or stewed together.
> — Randle Cotgrave, *A Dictionary of the French and English Tongues* (1611)

There's no accounting for taste of course, but making a room smell like a pot of boiling meat might not be the best way to freshen it up. Yet the English lexicographer Randle Cotgrave's definition — taken from what was at the time the largest and most ambitious bilingual dictionary in history — was not wrong. When it first appeared in the language in the early seventeenth century, a *potpourri* was a spiced stew, containing a mixture of meats and vegetables, not a collection of dried, perfumed flowers.

The name *potpourri* literally means 'rotten pot'. Although borrowed into English from French, it derives ultimately from an earlier Spanish term, *olla podrida* (which is a distant etymological relative of our word *putrid*). Quite why such an unappetising description should be given to a stew is unclear, but one theory claims that the meat-heavy stew might have formed an unsightly film of grease on its surface as it cooked and bubbled away, hence its fairly unattractive name. But whatever its origins might be, it was the dish's seemingly random assortment of ingredients that soon led to its name being used figuratively to describe any similar medley or random mixture of things.

In its native French, these mixed-up meanings were quick to emerge: by the turn of the seventeenth century, French speakers were using the name *potpourri* to refer to everything from musical medleys to literary anthologies, while as the name of an assortment of perfumed flowers, it first appeared in the late 1690s. In English, however, these figurative meanings were slow to catch on. It took until the mid 1700s for a fragranced *potpourri* of flowers to make its debut, followed by a musical *potpourri* mentioned in *The Times* newspaper in 1790. A literary *potpourri* finally found its way into the 1864 edition of Noah Webster's *American Dictionary*, defined as 'a literary production made up of parts brought together without order, or bond of connection'.

The change from 'assortment of stewed meat and vegetables' to 'random jumble or medley' might seem like an unusual one, but *potpourri* is by no means alone. The original *hodgepodge* or *hotch-potch*, for instance, was a *hochepot*, a medieval French stew thrown or 'hotched' together from minced beef and whatever vegetables were at hand. Similarly, when the word *gallimaufry* first appeared in the language in the late 1500s, one of its earliest meanings was as a byword for any dish pieced together from a hash of leftovers or odds and ends. And the word *salmagundi*, originally the name of a French dish of chopped meats, anchovies, boiled eggs and salad vegetables, has been used as another name for a random mixture of odds and ends since the mid 1700s – and in this sense was chosen by the American author Washington Irving as the name of the miscellaneous satirical magazine he founded in 1807.

Prestigious

originally meant 'deceitful'

When the word *prestige* first appeared in English in the mid seventeenth century, it originally referred to an illusion or a magic trick. Likewise the adjective *prestigious*, which made its debut a century earlier, originally described someone especially skilled in magic or sleight of hand. But when a conjuror performs some kind of magic trick – or else when some unsuspecting spectator falls for some kind of illusion – there is just as much guilefulness and deception at play as there is magic and clever showmanship, and because of that, neither *prestige* nor *prestigious* originally had entirely decent or positive connotations. In fact, both the modern use of *prestige* to mean 'respect' or 'esteem' and the modern use of *prestigious* to mean 'celebrated' or 'venerated' have somewhat darker pasts.

Prestige and *prestigious* derive ultimately from a Latin word, *praestigia*, which was used to mean both 'conjuror's tricks' or 'magic tricks', and 'trickery', 'deceit' or 'illusion'. It's likely that these negative implications were in place right from the very beginning, as the word *praestigia* itself is believed to come from an even earlier Latin word meaning 'to blindfold', or literally 'to bind the eyes'. These connotations were all carried through to English when both *prestige* and *prestigious* made their debuts in the language in the sixteenth and seventeenth centuries, as in this definition from an early English dictionary published in the mid 1600s:

> Prestiges: deceits, impostures, delusions, cousening [*cousining*] tricks.
>   — Thomas Blount, *Glossographia* (1656)

So how did we get from magic tricks and deception to esteem, respect and celebrity? It's tempting to credit this change in meaning to the impressiveness and effectiveness of a conjuror's tricks, which might have so captivated an audience that the conjuror or *prestigiator* himself was held in high regard. But regrettably, quite the opposite is probably the case as those negative connotations really just can't be ignored.

By the early nineteenth century, *prestigious* was beginning to be used to mean 'having an overawing or dazzling influence', while *prestige* now described influence or admiration that relied on past glories, or else disguised or excused faults or flaws:

> We feel with the young soldier his youthful admiration for Napoleon, and for all of which that name is a symbol; we see this enthusiasm die within him as the truth dawns upon him that this great man is an actor, that the prestige with which he overawed the

world is much if not in the largest portion of it the
effect of stage-trick.

— *The London and Westminster Review* (1838)

By the later 1800s, however, these negative and deceptive
associations had begun to disappear, so that by the turn
of the century *prestige* was merely 'high regard' or 'respect'.
Describing something or someone as *prestigious*, meanwhile,
implied nothing more than that they were well respected
or admired, and it is these meanings that have remained in
use ever since.

Punk

originally meant 'prostitute'

There's a line in Shakespeare's *Measure for Measure* in which
Mariana, the lonely and jilted ex-fiancée of Angelo, the deputy
of Vienna, is called 'a punk'. Moreover, in *All's Well that Ends
Well*, the Countess of Rossillon is contemptuously called a
'taffety punk'. Unsurprisingly, in both these lines Shakespeare
isn't implying that Mariana and the Countess have bleached
mohicans, piercings and leather jackets. Instead, he's using

the original sixteenth-century meaning of the word *punk* —
Mariana is being labelled a prostitute, while the Countess is
being dismissed as nothing more than a prostitute dressed
in taffeta, a fine silk fabric.

Frustratingly, no one is entirely sure where the word *punk*
comes from. Potential leads point everywhere from Spanish
expletives to wood-rotting fungi, to Scots dialect words for
the tired, dying embers of a fire, but none is entirely water-
tight and the word remains something of a mystery. What
is known, however, is that from its association with whores
and strumpets in sixteenth-century English, the word *punk*
embarked on quite a journey to reach its contemporary associations with punk rock in the late twentieth century. So
how did we get from there to here?

Building on Shakespeare's *punks*, by the seventeenth century
the meaning of the word had broadened to include men as
well as women who were involved in prostitution, and eventually, in the late 1600s, to young men in particular who
maintained sexual relationships with older men for monetary
or personal gain. *Punk* remained in use in these contexts
right through to the late nineteenth century, when it finally
began to be used much more generally of any disreputable
or contemptible person.

In this broader sense — which first emerged in American
slang before spreading elsewhere — *punk* was used not just of
prostitutes and gigolos, but petty thieves and pickpockets,

thugs and hooligans, yobs and yahoos. As time went by, other meanings and implications continued to emerge so that by the 1930s a *punk* could be anything from a naive, inexperienced new recruit to a coward or a weakling, and even a young animal born into the circus. But it was the word's seedy association with crime and disreputableness that survived the longest, so that by the 1960s *punk* was essentially a vaguely derogative term for someone up to no good:

> I know what you're thinking. 'Did he fire six shots, or only five?' Well, to tell you the truth, in all this excitement I kind of lost track myself . . . You've got to ask yourself a question: 'Do I feel lucky?' Well, do ya, punk?
>
> — *Dirty Harry* (1971)

It was in this sense that *punk* finally became attached to the rock-fuelled subculture of the early 1970s, and from there terms like *punk rock*, *punk pop* and *punk band* finally began to emerge towards the end of the twentieth century.

Queen

originally meant 'wife'

Emperors have *empresses*. Dukes have *duchesses*. Counts have *countesses*. Even mayors have *mayoresses*. So why is the wife of a king a *queen* and not a *kingess*?

Part of the reason for this apparent inconsistency is to do with how our society has operated throughout history. That fact that feminine equivalents of titles such as *emperor* and *duke* are so clearly derived from their male counterparts stems from the fact that, historically, gaining and maintaining ruling power and influence was an all but consistently male affair. The wives of emperors, dukes and counts were ultimately side-lined and kept back from having sway or authority, so the need for a separate title for a female marquess or a female viscount simply never came about. That being said, another part of the problem here stems from the meaning of the word *queen* itself.

Queen is actually one of the oldest recorded words we know of; instances of the Old English equivalent of 'queen', *cwen*, have been unearthed in documents dating as far back as the late ninth century. At that time, as well as meaning 'the wife of a king' (or, unlike today, 'the wife of a high-ranking nobleman'), *cwen* was also used to mean simply 'wife', and it's likely that this vague sense was the word's original meaning, which steadily became more specialised as the language changed. Precisely what sparked this development from 'wife' to 'wife of a king' is unclear — but it wasn't just *queen* that was affected along the way.

Whereas *queen* originally meant 'wife', the Old English word *wif* (as we saw under *man*) simply meant 'woman'. *Woman*, on the other hand, derives from the Old English *wifman*, or 'woman-man' (as we saw under *hussy*). Over time, *wifman* took the place of *wif*, and in turn *wif* took the place of *cwen*, which left *cwen* to become more specialised as a word for the wife of a nobleman or any equally high-ranking individual, and eventually the wife of a king. Which, if any, of these changes took place first, and precisely what sparked this gradual shift in the first place is unsure, but the entire change was complete by the end of the thirteenth century, and the word *queen* has remained in use with its current meaning ever since.

But that doesn't mean that this story ends here. As *wif* took over from *cwen*, *wifman* took over from *wif*, and *wife* gradually became the feminine counterpart of *husband*, another Old English word, *cwene*, drifted in the opposite direction. *Cwene* and *cwen* share a common root, but while *cwen* meant 'wife', *cwene* simply meant 'woman'. As *wifman* steadily took its place in the language, *cwene* picked up an array of negative and abusive connotations so that by the Middle Ages, *quean*, as it was now spelled, was being used to mean 'a brash, impudent woman', 'an immoral woman' and, finally, 'a prostitute' or 'bawd', the sense in which it too appeared in a number of Shakespeare's plays. Eventually the similarity between *queen* and *quean* became too confusing, and as other insults developed and began to take its place, *quean* finally all but disappeared from the language altogether.

Ragamuffin

was originally a demon

As a word for a tatty scrap of cloth, *rag* derives from a Scandinavian word for a shaggy or untidy tuft of hair or fur. On its own, it first appeared in written English in the early thirteenth century, but it was presumably in use long before then as Old English speakers had been describing things as *raggy* since the mid eleventh century at least. Shortly after its debut appearance, however, the word *rag* came to be used in a string of derivative words, all with a bizarre and somewhat unexpected association: *ragged*, *ragman* and *ragamuffin* all appeared within a hundred years of one another in the early Middle Ages – and all of them were originally used as nicknames for or descriptions of the Devil or one of his demons.

The word *ragged* was used to describe the Devil in a number of literary works dating as far back as the early 1300s, while the nickname *Ragman* remained in use right through to the 1500s. And when the word *ragamuffin* made its first appearance in the language in the Middle English allegorical poem *Piers Plowman*, it was as the name of one of the demons sired by 'Belial', a name for the Devil taken from the Hebrew Bible:

> Patriarchs and prophets have parled hereof long
> That such a lord and a light shall lead them all hence.
> But rise up, Ragamuffin! And reach me the bars
> That Belial thy bel-sire beat, with thy dame,
> And I shall let this lord and His light stop.
> — William Langland, *Piers Plowman* (*c.* 1376)

Like *ragged* and *ragman*, the 'rag' of *ragamuffin* is presumably meant to allude either to the Devil's shabby appearance, or else, based on the image of him having cloven hooves and the legs and tail of an animal, to his tatty, matted fur. The 'muffin' part, however, is harder to explain; Samuel Johnson famously had such a hard time trying to explain the etymology of *ragamuffin* when it came to compiling his *Dictionary of the English Language* (1755), that he simply wrote of its origin, 'from *rag*, and I know not what else'.

One theory is that the 'muffin' of *ragamuffin* is a corruption of an Old French word for an evil spirit or an objectionable person, *malfé*. Another claims that it might represent a mixture of English and French elements, *mal felon*. But confusing both of these ideas is the fact that the word might even have started out as a surname: an 'Isabella Ragamuffyn' is listed on a legal document from the city of Oxford in 1344. Was Isabella, or her family, so unpleasant that she was happy to be labelled 'mal felon'? Or was her surname a misspelling? An in-joke? A placeholder for a piece of missing information to be added later that was never corrected? No one knows for sure.

Whatever its origin might be, having started out as the name for some kind of hellish monster, the word *ragamuffin* steadily grew less severe, so that by the time it reappeared in the language in the late sixteenth century it was being used simply as a name for a dishevelled-looking or misbehaved person, and it is this meaning that has remained unchanged ever since.

Raunchy

originally meant 'dirty'

Nowadays when something (or someone) is described as *raunchy*, we tend to mean that it's provocative or suggestive, bawdy, or downright explicit. But, in more ways than one, things were a lot different in the 1930s:

> Raunchy – a name applied to anything that is dirty or in bad shape.

That definition comes from an edition of the American Air Corps newsletter published in 1939, which also explained that 'the flight commander's airplane' was nicknamed 'the washing machine', and that a drum major was called a 'regimental monkey'. But as for *raunchy*, that explanation is just about as far removed from modern *raunchiness* as it's possible to get. So how did it come about? And how did we get from there to the much more provocative meaning we have today?

The origins of *raunchy* are something of a mystery. There was an earlier dialect verb, *raunch* or *raunge*, in use in Britain in the eighteenth and nineteenth centuries meaning 'to devour greedily' or 'to munch' or 'gnaw', but it seems unlikely that a word could find its way from eighteenth-century England and parachute its way into the pre-Second World War American Air Corps with no trace of it recorded in between. A much more likely idea is that it might be derived from a Mexican Spanish word, *rancho*, which was in use in nineteenth-century America as another name for a farmstead or collection of outbuildings (and is the origin of the word *ranch*) but eventually came to have somewhat negative connotations – perhaps through association with something being spoiled or marked with waste from livestock:

> RANCHO, originally a Spanish-American word, signifying a hunting-lodge, or cattle-station, in a wood or desert far from the haunts of men . . . In Washington, with their accustomed ingenuity in corrupting words and meanings, the Americans used the appellation for a place of evil report.
> – John Camden Hotten, *The Slang Dictionary* (1864)

No matter what its origin might be, *raunchy* made its debut in the slang of the American military in the mid 1930s and continued to be used to mean 'dirty', 'shabby' or 'unkempt' – and, by extension, 'slovenly' or 'inept' – for several decades to come.

It was presumably through its connection to dirtiness and slovenliness that by the 1940s *raunchy* was beginning to be used to describe anything unrefined, unsophisticated or rough and ready, and by the 1960s this meaning had developed to mean 'coarse', 'brazen' or 'unabashed', and eventually 'lewd', 'suggestive' and 'explicit'. The word, and this meaning, has remained unchanged ever since.

ℛefrigerator

was originally an antipyretic medicine

In an essay on *A Method of Discovering the Virtues of Plants* written for the Royal Society in 1722, the astronomer and scientist Edmond Halley outlined a system of categorising all the plants at that time known to have medicinal value. The first of his categories comprised all those known to be useful in what he euphemistically termed 'altering and evacuating' the body, which he in turn divided into those consisting of 'gross particles' and those consisting of 'subtle particles':

> Those consisting of gross particles are astringent. Such as prevent . . . diarrhoea, dysentery; good in burnings, bruises, cancers, spitting of blood. Gross medicines are narcotics, vulnerary, good for scrofulous tumours, squinancy, refrigerators.
>
> — *Philosophical Transactions* (1722)

So alongside being good for healing wounds ('vulnerary') and bacterial infection of the tonsils ('squinancy'), Halley's 'gross medicines' were also 'good for refrigerators' – and no prizes for guessing he wasn't talking about that thing in your kitchen.

The word *refrigerator* first appeared in English in the early seventeenth century, although the verb from which it is derived, *refrigerate*, dates back another hundred years and the process of *refrigeration* first emerged in the late 1400s. Back then, as it still does today, *refrigeration* meant simply 'the action of freezing, cooling or making cold'; at its centre is the Latin word *frigus*, meaning 'cold', from which the adjective *frigid* likewise derives. But unlike today, *refrigeration* was originally a medical term, referring to the easing of a fever, the relief of an inflammation, or the reduction of a swelling or distension. The *refrigerator* mentioned by Halley, then, was actually an antipyretic or fever-reducing medicine.

This medical meaning remained in place right through to the twentieth century and is still occasionally used in medical jargon today – but in the early eighteenth century, things began to change. Thanks to a series of technological developments, in the 1700s the word *refrigerator* began to be applied to devices and processes, both mechanical and chemical, that either reduce or absorb heat. Over the years that followed, it came to be variously used of a piece of laboratory equipment used to condense vapours, a vat used to cool the 'mashed' or grain-infused liquid (the wort) in a brewery, and a coil of tubing containing cold water that was used to cool early hot-air engines. Finally, in the early 1800s, the refrigerator we know today began to take shape.

A description of a 'newly invented machine called the refrigerator' was published in 1803, and as the technology improved and domestic refrigerators became more common-place – replacing the older and much less convenient 'ice-houses' used to store and produce ice in Victorian house-holds – all earlier meanings of the word drifted into obscurity. The abbreviation *fridge* emerged shortly afterwards, in the late 1920s, before the first *fridge-freezer* appeared in 1971.

Sad

originally meant 'satisfied'

The Latin word for 'enough' or 'ample', *satis*, is the origin of a host of English words, each carrying some similar sense of sufficiency or adequacy. *Satiate*, for instance, has been used to mean 'fully gratified or filled' since the early fifteenth century. The same goes for *saturate*, and *satisfy*, which literally means 'to do enough' but originally meant 'to pay off a debt' when it first appeared in English in the mid 1400s. Likewise your *assets* are quite literally all those belongings valuable enough to cover the cost of your debts, while *satire* originally referred to a medley of different written works or writing styles and takes its name from a Roman fruit salad called *lanx satura*, or 'full dish'. And then, derived from precisely the same roots as all of these, there's *sad* – and as journeys through the language go, *sad* has been on quite the satisfying one.

As a derivative of *satis*, when *sad* first appeared in the language in the Old English period it was used to mean 'satisfied', 'sated' or 'having had your fill'. Frankly, being fully satisfied might not sound like the saddest feeling in the world, but that's not to say that the negative connotations of *sad* were slow to appear: by the early Middle Ages, it was already being used to mean 'heavy-hearted', 'wearied', 'worn down', in the sense of being subjected to or made to endure too much of something that has consequently become insufferable. But the word wasn't done yet.

From there *sad* began to gain connotations of ponderousness and heaviness, in the related sense of literally being weighed down by an unbearable excess of something. By the turn of the fourteenth century *sad* was being used to mean 'weighty', 'solid', 'compacted' and 'resistant' (solid, unworkable soils are still sometimes designated *sad* in horticultural contexts), and later 'steadfast', 'reliable', 'trustworthy' and 'genuine'. But if you think that's all starting to sound quite positive again, don't worry — those negative connotations just kept on coming.

Building on its association with steadfastness and solidity, *sad* then came to mean 'dignified' and 'sober', and from there began to mean 'grave', 'serious' and 'solemn'. Finally, these new meanings, combined with the word's earlier associations with weariness and heavy-heartedness, all conspired to provide *sad* with its now familiar meaning of 'sorrowful', 'glum', 'despondent' and 'unhappy' by the turn of the fifteenth century. All earlier positive connotations steadily disappeared over time, leaving the word's negative meaning to stand alone by the 1600s and *sad* has remained all but unchanged ever since. Well, almost.

Thanks to the consistently inventive world of slang, in the twentieth century *sad* finally came to be used to mean 'pathetic', 'inadequate' and, by extension, 'unfashionable', 'out of touch' and 'out of date'. Derivative insults, like *sad-sack* and *sad-case*, began to emerge too, each one doled out to some hopelessly inept or inadequate person. As modern as all this might feel, however, the use of *sad* to mean 'unfashionable' or 'undesirable' is actually almost a hundred years old:

'Philosophy's rather highbrow at college. If you go in
for that kind of thing, they think you're rather sad.'
    'Rather what?' I said.
    'Oh, sad is a technical term; it's the opposite of tops.'
        — Irwin Edman, *Philosopher's Holiday* (1938)

Secretary

originally meant 'keeper of secrets'

So by now we know that *girls* could once be boys. *Bimbos* were men. *Algebra* can mend your broken bones. People were once *exploded* from the stage. It's fair to say that some of the changes of meaning on this list are rather unexpected – but on the other hand, there are those words on this list whose histories and origins have been staring you in the face the entire time but just never fell into place. *Blockbusters* originally 'busted blocks'. *Cupboards* were originally 'boards' for your 'cups'. And *secretaries* originally kept your secrets.

The word *secretary* was borrowed into English from its Latin equivalent, *secretarius*, which was used in the medieval period as a general term for a clerk, a notary or a scribe. At its centre is the Latin word for 'secret', *secretum*, as part of the role of these medieval clerks was to keep the confidential information their employers and superiors entrusted them with absolutely secret.

In this sense, the Latin *secretarius* was first in use in England as far back as the mid thirteenth century as the title of an officer of the royal court whose job involved organising and dealing with the king's correspondence – a role that understandably involved a great deal of keeping or covering up state secrets. The earliest king's secretary we know about was Sir John Maunsell, who is known to have held the title of *secretarius noster*, literally 'our secretary', while serving as chancellor under King Henry III in the mid thirteenth century.

By the late fourteenth century, however, the Latin title *secretarius* had been fully adopted into English as *secretary* and began to be used simply as another word for a close confidant, or else someone entrusted with some kind of private matter. This clandestine meaning survived right through to the late 1500s, before the principal meaning we use it for today – namely, an assistant, or administrative office worker – began to take centre stage. But to find out how that meaning came about, we need to return to the court of King Henry III.

Besides keeping the king's secrets and dealing with his correspondence, Maunsell's job as *secretarius* was also a diplomatic one: in 1253 he was sent to Spain to help negotiate a peace treaty, and the following year he helped broker the marriage of Henry's son and heir, Prince Edward, to Eleanor of Castile. Over the centuries that followed, the role of king's secretary became increasingly organisational, political and powerful, so that by the end of the Tudor period, Elizabeth I became the first monarch to appoint an official Secretary of State (or 'Secretary of Estate', as it was back then) in late 1580s. By this time many of

England's ambassadors, knights, noblemen and all the other high-society figures of the day had seen first hand the benefit of having a close personal assistant to help organise their affairs, and so by the turn of the seventeenth century the term *secretary* was being used both in the political sense of an official appointed government minister, and in the broader sense of simply a personal clerical assistant:

> Secretary, one that is employ'd in writing letters, dispatches, &c. for a prince, nobleman, or particular society: also one that attends upon an ambassador, envoy, or resident for that purpose. The King's Secretaries, certain officers that sign the Dispatches of the Seal.
>
> – *The New World of Words,*
> *or a Universal Dictionary* (1706)

And it is from their work, assisting the ambassadors and noblemen of the late Middle Ages, that all our *secretaries* have since taken their job title.

Shampoo

was originally a massage

In an account of *A Voyage to the West Indies* published in 1762, an unknown 'officer in the service of the East India Company' wrote the earliest known description of seemingly one of the most everyday of activities:

> Shampooing is an operation not known in Europe . . . which I once had the curiosity to go through, and for which I paid but a trifle . . . He [*the shampooer*] first placed me in a large chair; then began to beat with both his hands very fast upon all parts of my body. He next stretched out my arms and legs, and gave them several sudden pulls that racked my joints; then he got my arm upon his shoulder, and hauled me sideways a good way over the chair; and as suddenly gave my head a twitch or jerk round that I thought he should have put my neck out of joint.

If you're thinking that that description doesn't sound like any *shampoo* you've ever used, you'd be quite right. That's because when it first appeared in the language in the mid eighteenth century, *shampoo* was another name for what we'd now call a massage.

The word *shampoo* was brought to English attention by explorers and merchants who travelled and traded their way around Asia at the height of the colonial era. The word itself derives from *čampo*, a Hindi word literally meaning 'press' or 'squeeze', which in turn probably has its origins in an even older Sanskrit word meaning 'to knead' or 'pound'. But how did we get from an intense (and somewhat painful-sounding) full body massage to a word meaning 'to wash the hair'?

Although the author of the extract above makes no mention of it, traditional Indian massages like these typically involved the use of fragrant soaps and lathers that would be used to cleanse both the skin and the hair of the person being massaged. British and European colonialists living in India who had acquired a liking for these kinds of treatments brought their experiences back to Europe when they returned home, and with them came the word *shampoo*. Over time, the association between shampooing and massaging steadily disappeared, a demise no doubt hastened by the naturally more reserved Brits – and the even more reserved Victorians at that, who likely did not share the colonialists' enthusiasm for being rubbed and pummelled while near naked. Ultimately, by the mid nineteenth century *shampoo* had begun to be used all but exclusively to refer to washing and fragrancing the hair, with the earliest reference to a cleansing detergent or 'wash' being called a *shampoo* dating from 1838.

Skulduggery

was originally illegal lewdness

It's tempting to think that as another word for disreputable, devious behaviour – and with its subtle nod towards the word *skull* – *skulduggery* might have some kind of connection to the swashbuckling behaviour of pirates and buccaneers. In fact, there's no such connection at all; it's a lot more bizarre than that.

Skulduggery first appeared in the language, with its modern sense and spelling, in the mid 1800s, with its earliest record appearing in an American newspaper in 1867 that described it as a 'mysterious term . . . used to signify political or other trickery'. Before then, however, *skulduggery* was *sculduddery*, an old Scots dialect word that nineteenth-century lexicographer John Jamieson defined as:

> A term, now used in a ludicrous manner, to denote those causes that come under the judgement of an ecclesiastical court, which respect some breach of chastity.
>
> — John Jamieson, *An Etymological Dictionary of the Scottish Language* (1808)

So *skulduggery* – or rather *sculduddery* – seemingly began life as a legal term referring to any crime or misdemeanour that comprised a 'breach of chastity' in the eyes of Scotland's strict Presbyterian courts. In that sense, the term has been unearthed as far back as 1663, in a letter written by the Earl of Argyll to Sir Archibald Primrose, the Clerk-Register of the Scottish court, in which he mentions that an unnamed acquaintance has been arrested 'not for sculdudry . . . but for a less gentlemanny crime, theft'. Theft carried the threat of the death penalty at that time, and the Earl was writing to the clerk-register to request leniency in passing sentence. The 'more gentlemanny' crime of *sculduddery* carried a less severe – if more humiliating – penalty, as explained in another letter dated 1730:

> If any one be brought before a presbytery to be questioned for sculduddery, i.e. fornication or adultery . . . the offender . . . will be avoided by his friends, acquaintance, and all that know him . . . I was told in Edinburgh of a certain Scots colonel, being convicted of adultery . . . was sentenced to stand in a hair cloth at the kirk door every Sunday morning for a whole year, and to this he submitted. At the beginning of his penance he concealed his face as much as he could, but three or four young lasses passing by him, one of them stooped down, and cried out to her companions, 'Lord! it's Colonel – – .' Upon which he suddenly threw aside his disguise, and said, 'Miss, you are right; and

if you will be the subject of it, I will wear this coat another twelvemonth.'
— Edward Burt, *Letters from a Gentleman in the North of Scotland* (1754)

Whether this anecdote is true or not, it shows that the legal definition of *sculduddery* was still in place by the mid 1700s, but the fact that John Jamieson, compiling his dictionary just after the turn of the nineteenth century, pointed out that *sculduddery* is 'now used in a ludicrous manner' suggests that this meaning had already weakened by the early 1800s. Indeed, by the 1820s *sculduddery* had become little more than a byword for obscenity or vulgarity, and it's from there that the modern sense of 'disreputable behaviour' or 'dishonesty' — and eventually the modern spelling *skulduggery* — emerged in the mid nineteenth century.

Slogan

was originally a war cry

It is all too easy — and not to mention somewhat unfair — to think that the Irish contribution to the English language starts at *shamrocks* and ends at *leprechauns*. But in fact, Irish is responsible for a great many more English words than it might appear, including several surprisingly familiar everyday words whose Irish origins and association with Irish culture might not be so immediately obvious.

Trousers, for instance, take their name from a type of knee-length breeches originally known by the Irish name *triubhas*. *Galore* comes from *go leor*, an Irish expression literally meaning 'enough' or 'sufficient'. When you call someone a *slob*, you're literally comparing them to ooze or slime, or an area of boggy marshland known in Irish as *slaba*. Even the British *Tory* party takes its name (albeit via a few political and etymological twists and turns) from *tóraidhe*, an Irish word for an outlaw or plunderer – a word disparagingly applied by the Whigs in the late 1600s to all those politicians who opposed the Exclusion Bill (that sought to exclude Charles II's Catholic brother, the Duke of York, from the throne). And then there's *slogan*, whose origins lie far detached from the worlds of advertising and political promotion, and on the ancient battlefields of Scotland.

The original *slogan* was a battle cry or war cry, and the word itself derives from a corruption of *sluagh-ghairm*, a Gaelic compound that brings together the words for 'army', *sluagh*, and 'cry' or 'shout', *ghairm*. Like many old Gaelic-origin words, it's difficult to tell whether this *slogan* was originally an Irish or a Scots word: on its first appearance in English in the sixteenth century, it was particularly associated with the clans and peoples of the Scottish Highlands and Borderlands, but as this region had long been occupied by Irish settlers and invaders, it's very possible the word might have been brought to Britain from across the Irish Sea.

Wherever its geographical origins might lie, however, the very first *slogans* typically comprised little more than a nearby place name, or the surname of some local leader or chieftain that would be rousingly bellowed across the battlefields of Scotland. And it's in this military context that the word *slogan* first appeared in English in the early 1500s.

Slogan remained in use in this sense for the next 300 years, until its appearance in the works of writers like Sir Walter Scott (as well as the popularity in general of Scottish literature and poetry in the nineteenth century) brought it to a wider audience. By the mid 1800s, *slogan* was being used much more generally as just another name for a motto or dictum associated with some political or social movement, before the very first advertising *slogans* began to appear in the early twentieth century. Finally, the word's warlike origins fell out of use, save for in military and historical contexts, leaving the *slogan's* association with advertising and rabble-rousing politics in place to this day.

Snob

originally meant 'cobbler'

There's a popular myth that claims the word *snob* derives from the Latin phrase *sine nobilitate*, 'without nobility'. If the stories are to be believed, the abbreviation '*s. nob.*' was once used on anything from census reports to lists of university admissions, to designate all those individuals with no connection to the aristocracy or nobility. It's an ingenious theory, but entirely untrue — not least because no such abbreviation has ever been spotted in admission records or censuses. The word *snob* itself, moreover, actually began life as an eighteenth-century word for a cobbler.

In his *Classical Dictionary of the Vulgar Tongue* (1785), Francis Grose defined the word *snob* as 'a nickname for a shoemaker'. No one is entirely sure where the word originated, and although one theory suggests that it might come from the name of some ancient piece of cobbling equipment, no such tool has ever been discovered. Whatever its origins, as another name for a shoemaker *snob* vanished from the language around a century later, but in the decades between it had embarked on quite an etymological journey.

Around the turn of the nineteenth century, just a few decades after Grose's dictionary was published, *snob* began to be used among students at Cambridge University as a slang name for a 'townsman', namely a resident of Cambridge who did not attend the university. A few years after that, it was in use more generally to refer to someone of a relatively low social standing, with little breeding or taste, or (as in the *sine nobilitate* myth) without any connection to rank or nobility. In all these instances, it's likely that the traditional occupation of shoemaker or 'snob' had simply been singled out as a stereotypically lowly, manual and unacademic profession. But to modern English speakers, this might all seem a little backward. Surely disparaging someone's lack of a university education makes you the *snob*, not the other way around?

Well, everything began to change in the mid 1800s, when the language started to reflect the desire of the lowly, uneducated *snobs* of the early nineteenth century to improve their social standing – or, at least, to give the impression that they were of greater status than they truly were. This meaning had seemingly already established itself by the time William Makepeace Thackeray published his *Book of Snobs*, a collection of satirical articles and essays, in 1848:

> The word Snob has taken a place in our honest English vocabulary. We can't define it, perhaps. We can't say what it is, any more than we can define wit, or humour, or humbug; but we KNOW what it is. Some weeks

since, happening to have the felicity to sit next to a young lady at a hospitable table, where poor old Jawkins was holding forth in a very absurd pompous manner, I wrote upon the spotless damask 'S – B', and called my neighbour's attention to the little remark. That young lady smiled. She knew it at once. Her mind straightway filled up the two letters concealed by apostrophic reserve, and I read in her assenting eyes that she knew Jawkins was a Snob.

Thackeray's essays characterised the Victorian *snob* as a blustering, pretentious, bragging elitist, who professes to know much about important subjects, mistreats those of lower social standing, and ingratiates themselves with those above them. To describe this behaviour, he invented the word *snobbishness* (although Dickens had already used the word *snobbish* in 1841), and it's this image of a snooty, arrogant *snob* that has remained in place ever since.

Sophisticated

originally meant 'contaminated'

The word *sophistication* has long had associations with knowledge and learning, it's just that they've not always been good. Back in Ancient Greece, the Sophists (who took their name from a Greek word meaning 'wisdom') were itinerant teachers and philosophers, who would travel from place to place giving lessons on anything from politics to rhetoric to art to public speaking – a combination of disciplines they called *arete*, meaning 'virtue' or 'excellence'. The Sophists believed that true knowledge was all but unattainable, and that the process of articulating your point of view was more important than its informedness or reasoning. This stance, allied with the fact that they charged for their services and so were typically hired by only the wealthiest citizens to improve their chances of rising to public office, put the Sophists in direct opposition to the likes of Socrates, his students Xenophon and Plato, and Plato's own student Aristotle. They railed against the Sophists, condemning their actions as deceitful and deceptive. Plato in particular depicted them as paid hunters of impressionable young men, and dismissed them as the travelling salesmen of learning and imitators of the wise.

Based on these scathing portrayals, a Latin word *sophistria* emerged in the medieval period to refer to specious, fallacious or tainted reasoning. Alongside that, a verb *sophisticare* developed, which was used to mean 'to adulterate', or 'to tamper with something dishonestly'. The former eventually gave us the word *sophistry* in the mid 1300s; the latter gave us the word *sophisticate* in the early fifteenth century.

Sophisticate was originally a verb, used to mean 'to contaminate something by mixing it with something inferior'; something that was *sophisticated*, ultimately, was contaminated, adulterated or impure. In particular, these words were applied to dishonest tradesmen and merchants who would bulk out expensive commodities with substandard or even entirely fake material. The earliest written record of this kind of trick refers to pepper (a rare and enormously expensive spice in the Middle Ages) being 'sophisticated', but almost every commodity from alcohol to medicines was liable to be tampered with: tobacco was mixed with wood shavings, honey was bulked out with castor oil, tea with dried leaves and grass, coffee with roasted acorns. By the nineteenth century, *sophisticated* produce was everywhere. But at what point did the modern meaning of *sophisticated* begin to emerge? Well, the answer to that lies in its opposite.

Around the turn of the seventeenth century, the adjective *unsophisticated* was being used to refer to anything that had *not* been tainted or tampered with. By the mid 1600s, that meaning had become more figurative, so that *unsophisticated* had come to mean 'naive', 'ingenuous' and 'uninformed'. In return, *its* opposite began to be used to mean the opposite of that, so that by the late nineteenth century, *sophisticated* was finally being used to mean 'informed', 'experienced' and 'worldly-wise'. As the association between *sophistication* and education, refinement and high culture continued to build, the older meaning fell by the etymological wayside, leaving us with the word *sophisticated* as it is today.

Success

originally meant 'outcome', either good or bad

Nothing, we are told, succeeds like success. It's a nice motto to live by certainly, implying that hard work pays off and has the potential to lead to bigger and better successes in the future. It's just a shame that, etymologically at least, it doesn't make a great deal of sense.

Words like *succeed*, *success* and *successful* can all be traced back to the Latin verb *succedere*, meaning 'to advance' or 'to follow'. It in turn is built around the verb *cedere*, meaning simply 'to go', 'to yield to' or 'to proceed'. English is chock-full of derivatives of *cedere* – you'll find it listed in the histories of words such as *predecessor* and *antecedent, accession* and *concession, exceed* and *concede,* and *excess* and *recess,* to name but a few – the majority of which, including *succeed* itself, first appeared in the early Middle Ages.

The earliest meaning of *succeed* in English is one that still survives today: 'to come next in order', 'to be the immediate successor or follower' or 'to take the place of'. We still talk of people *succeeding* others into office and monarchs *succeeding* each other to the throne, and this general sense of *succeeding* was carried through to the word *success* when it first emerged in the early 1500s. Originally, it simply referred to any outcome or upshot, or to any subsequent state of affairs, regardless of whether it was positive or negative:

EROS: There's strange news come, sir.
ENOBARBUS: What, man?
EROS: Caesar and Lepidus have made wars upon Pompey.
ENOBARBUS: This is old. What is the success?
                                    – William Shakespeare,
                        Antony and Cleopatra, III.v (*c.* 1604)

Because *successes* in sixteenth- and seventeenth-century English could be either good or bad, they typically had to be qualified as such in their context. The *success* in *Antony and Cleopatra,* we soon discover is not a good one: Lepidus has been imprisoned by Caesar, leaving him and Marc Antony alone, locked in battle. But elsewhere in Shakespeare he mentions a 'good success', an 'ill success' and even a 'vile success', each one describing a different kind of positive or negative outcome. Saying that 'nothing succeeds like success', ultimately, would once just have meant something like 'nothing happens like things that happen'.

By the late 1500s, however, *success* was beginning to be used without the need for any elucidating context to imply a positive accomplishment or outcome. Precisely why this positive meaning should have won over all others is unclear, but whatever sparked it, this change in meaning had all but fully established itself by the mid nineteenth century, and *successes* have remained resolutely successful ever since.

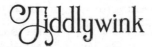

Tiddlywink

originally meant 'unlicensed pub'

One of the earliest recorded references to a *tiddlywink* in English dates from 1844 – in which it is fairly uncompromisingly accused of having the ability to be a person's downfall:

Such is a brief sketch of the nature and objects of this most abominable business *[hire purchase]*, which does more to demoralize and ruin the lower classes than a Tom and Jerry, tidley-wink, or gin-shop.

— Joseph Hewlett, *Parsons and Widows* (1844)

Does a colourful counter used to flip other colourful counters into a cup really have the potential to ruin someone? Never say never, of course, but it's unlikely. Instead, the *tiddlywink* being mentioned here is nothing like the *tiddlywinks* we know today.

In Victorian slang, a *tiddlywink* was an unlicensed or downmarket pub. Aside from the fact that *tiddly* has been used as a euphemism for being drunk (and before that for an alcoholic drink itself) since the early nineteenth century, there's little etymological evidence to go on here and the word's precise origins remain a mystery. One theory maintains that *tiddly* might have begun life as a jocular, deliberately childish pronunciation of 'little', which perhaps in combination with the old-fashioned use of *wink* to mean 'a brief amount of time' or 'a tiny amount' (as in 'I haven't slept a wink!') might imply that the original *tiddlywink* was a quick tipple, or a mouthful of drink — or else somewhere where just such a restorative could be purchased. That's just a theory, of course, and with so little evidence to go on it's impossible to decide whether there's much truth to it. In fact, in a fine example of an etymological the-chicken-or-the-egg problem, it could be that *tiddly* derives from *tiddlywink* rather than the other way around, which would cast doubt on this entire idea. No matter where its origins might lie, however, by the mid 1850s *tiddlywink* was already being used as the name of a bar game – but even then, it wasn't the game we know today.

Originally, *tiddlywink* was a variation of dominoes that according to *Routledge's Every Boy's Annual* (1870) involved 'four, six or eight players' who, unlike in a normal game of dominoes, each have the right to a second go after playing a double; the game ends when 'the one who first plays out all his dominoes calls "tidley-wink"'. By the 1890s however, this game had fallen out of fashion, and the game of *tiddlywinks* as we know it today quickly took its place – although it was apparently a lot more exciting back then than it is today:

> After dinner we all played the most exciting game that ever was invented, called Tiddleywinks. It consists of flipping counters into a bowl, and being a good number we played at two tables, one table against another, and the excitement was tremendous. I assure you that everyone's character changes at Tiddleywinks in the most marvellous way. To begin with, everyone begins to scream at the top of their voices and to accuse everyone else of cheating. Even I forgot my shyness and howled with excitement . . . I assure you,

no words can picture either the intense excitement or
the noise. I almost scream in describing it.

    – Lady Emily Lytton, to Reverend Whitwell Elwin,

24 April 1892

*T*it for Tat

originally meant 'you hit me, I'll hit you'

When we do something *tit for tat*, we do it as part of an
exchange or retaliation. But what exactly are (in this context
as least) a *tit* and a *tat*? And why should you be looking to
trade one for the other?

It is tempting to think that in relation to a back-and-forth,
one-for-the-other exchange, *tit* and *tat* might simply derive
from *this* and *that*. It's certainly true that these two began
life as entirely different words – but not those. Instead,
tit for tat is thought to have begun life as *tip for tap*, an
expression that has since been unearthed as far back as
the fifteenth century.

In this context, a *tip* is a strike or blow, or a light knock
or impact. It derives directly from the even older use of *tip*
as a verb, meaning 'to knock' or 'to touch', which likely dates

back to the Middle English period. A *tap* is essentially the same: a light rap or blow, and it too derives from the earlier use of *tap* as a verb that has been used to mean 'to rap' or 'to knock lightly' since the early thirteenth century. Both words were probably coined onomatopoeically.

When put together, that means *tip for tap* originally meant 'blow for blow' — or, in other words, 'you hit me, I'll hit you'. By the mid 1500s this had morphed into *tit for tat*, but retained this fairly uncompromising sense of revenge, or eye-for-an-eye retaliation:

> Spiders, quoth the ant, take those customs far unlike,
> Theirs to grow of right, flies' of usurpation.
> If, quoth the butterfly, the flies do here pike
> That quarrel to spiders, in custom's usation,
> That is tit for tat in this altercation.
> So that for any thing any party can get,
> Both parties in all things yet on even hand are set.
> — John Heywood,
> 'The Spider and the Flie' (1556)

The meaning of *tit for tat* has changed relatively little since then, except that today it tends to be used in a weaker sense less concerned with revenge, and more with cooperation, reciprocity, and ensuring a fair trade or swap. The earlier associations with retribution and a give-as-good-as-you-get mentality might not have disappeared entirely, but since the early nineteenth century *tit for tat* has been increasingly used in more positive contexts to refer to mutually beneficial, quid pro quo arrangements, where advice, assistance or some other exchangeable commodity is offered reciprocally by two parties.

Treadmill

was originally a prison punishment

Depending on what your opinions are of exercise, the fact that there is any kind of connection between gym equipment and hard labour in a Victorian prison might come as little surprise. But, oddly, that's precisely where the word *treadmill* fits into the language – and to understand why, we have to go back to eighteenth-century England.

The engineer William Cubitt was born in Norfolk in 1785. The son of a local miller, he grew up in a predominantly agricultural community and dedicated much of his early life – and his unending enthusiasm for design and invention – to producing new and ever more efficient machinery to ease the tough manual labour he had grown up around.

Indeed Cubitt's long list of inventions included everything from a new design for an agricultural thresher, to a set of self-regulating windmill sails.

In later life, Cubitt moved to London and applied his knowledge to much larger engineering projects, including canals, bridges, railways and docks; the Oxford canal, the old coal-loading docks at the mouth of the River Tees and part of the London to Brighton railway line are all examples of his work. In 1830, he was made a fellow of the Royal Society and in 1850 was elected president of the Institute of Civil Engineers, a position that eventually led to his involvement in the construction of the Crystal Palace in Hyde Park, for the Great Exhibition the following year. For his contribution to the project, Cubitt was knighted by Queen Victoria in December 1851. But from amidst this lifetime of innovation and accomplishment, one of Cubitt's inventions stands out above all others: in 1818, he invented the treadmill.

According to legend, Cubitt happened one day to notice the prisoners in one of London's gaols merely idling their time away in the prison yard. Sensing a wasted opportunity, he conceived of a device that would not only stir them from their lassitude and allow them to pass their time in prison more actively, but could harness this activity to provide a useful service – albeit an arduous and unpleasant one. The design he came up with involved an enormous cylinder, surrounded by a series of loops or belts, each fitted at regular intervals with steps or rungs. Pushing down on the first step with your foot would move the belt around the cylinder, and bring another step around to take its place, essentially forming a never-ending staircase; in a gruelling eight-hour shift, a prisoner stepping in this manner would climb the equivalent of more than 7,000ft. This huge man-powered mill could then be adapted or connected up to some other piece of machinery, harnessing the men's labour to do anything from grinding grain to crushing rocks to produce grit for the construction industry.

Cubitt initially referred to his invention as the 'tread-wheel', but in a description published in 1822 it is referred to as 'the tread mill invented by Mr William Cubitt of Ipswich, for the employment of prisoners'. And this – a hard-labour punishment in Victorian gaols – was the first recorded *treadmill* in the English language.

Cubitt's treadmills remained in use in English prisons right through to the turn of the century, when prison reform and the increasing industrialisation of society made the work the prisoners were performing a thing of the past. As they disappeared, so too did the word *treadmill* itself, until it was rescued from obscurity in the 1950s – during the post-war vogue for fitness and exercise – and applied to a piece of gym equipment that used a similarly unending, foot-powered rotating belt. Although which of the two provides the less pleasant experience is up to you to decide.

ℰUnhappy

originally meant 'unlucky'

It might not seem like it, but words such as *happy* and *unhappy*, *hapless*, *haphazard* and *happenchance* are all related. At their centre is *hap*, a word that was in use in the language by the early thirteenth century to mean 'fortune' or 'luck', but has now long since fallen out of common use. Just like *success*, whether *hap* referred to good luck or bad luck typically depended on the context in which it appeared. But a handful of more specific derivatives, making it clear what kind of fortune was implied, were quick to appear.

The first *mishap*, for instance, took place in the early 1200s, while its little used opposite, *goodhap*, did not emerge until the sixteenth century. If you're *hapless*, you literally have no luck at all; it appeared in the early 1400s, but by the twentieth century its original meaning had altered slightly, to 'clumsy' or 'incompetent'. Things have been *haphazard* since the mid 1500s, a term that literally implies surrendering all control over chance or accident. And the verb *happen* literally means 'to occur by hap' – or, in other words, 'to occur either by chance, or by good or bad fortune' – before the more general meaning of 'to take place' or 'to come to pass' developed later. Its associations with luck and fortuitousness re-emerged in the nineteenth century, thanks to derivatives such as *happen-chance* and *happenstance*.

Luck and chance are also at the centre of *happy* and *unhappy*. Both words appeared in the language in the fourteenth century — before then, if you happened to be 'happy' in Old English, you would have had to describe yourself as either *gesælig* (a word that eventually morphed into *silly*) or else *bliðe* (which eventually became *blithe*). Of the two, oddly *unhappy* has been discovered the furthest back in time: it appears in the *Cursor Mundi* or 'Runner of the World', an enormous Middle English poem written sometime around 1300 that refers at one point to an 'unhappy wretch'. *Happy* meanwhile has only been traced as far back as 1387 and an English translation of a Latin religious chronicle, the *Polychronicon*, in which King Herod is described as 'most ungracious in homely things, and happy in other things'.

That's not to mean that Herod is smiling contentedly over his 'other things', of course, nor that the 'wretch' in the *Cursor Mundi* is bawling his eyes out in sadness. Instead, *happy* originally meant 'lucky', while *unhappy* meant 'unlucky' or 'unfortunate' — or, quite literally, 'without hap'.

Although this association between happiness and luck can still be felt today when we talk of 'happy coincidences' or 'unhappy accidents', by the fifteenth century things had started to change. Presumably because having fortune on your side is more favourable a situation, *happy* began to be used to mean 'contented', 'satisfied' or 'glad', while *unhappy* began to be used to mean 'miserable', 'wretched' and, eventually, 'sad' and 'despondent', presumably because having no luck at all is such an unfavourable situation. Over the centuries that followed, other meanings came and went (*happy* once also meant 'dextrous', *unhappy* once meant 'unsuccessful' and 'ominous') though none survived for long, leaving *happy* and *unhappy*, in the sense of 'glad' and 'sad', the opposites we have today.

Venom

was originally a love potion

Would you rather come across a poisonous snake, or a venomous snake? It might sound like there's little difference between the two (and the correct answer is, of course, that you'd rather not come across any snake at all), but despite being used all but interchangeably today, the words *poisonous* and *venomous* actually have subtly different meanings.

Strictly speaking, *poisonous* creatures produce or secrete their harmful chemicals throughout their bodies or through their skin, and so are only dangerous should you ever feel the need to touch one or eat one. *Venomous* creatures, on the other hand, need to inject their toxins in order to harm you, and so are only dangerous if they happen to bite you, or if their venom somehow manages to enter your bloodstream through an open cut or wound. And then there are those creatures that are both poisonous *and* venomous, but frankly that's a zoological road that nobody wants to go down.

Etymologically, this toxic distinction isn't actually mirrored by the words' histories (nor by the word *toxic* for that matter, which has its roots in the Ancient Greek word for an archer's bow, *toxos*, and perhaps originally referred to some harmful substance smeared on the tips of arrows). Both *poison* and *venom* originally meant merely 'poisonous substance', but while *poison* itself derives from the Latin verb *potare*, meaning 'to drink', *venom* has a trick up its sleeve. It derives from *venenum*, another Latin word used not only to mean 'poison', but also 'medicine', 'drug', 'charm' and even 'magic potion' – and all these connotations have led to suggestions that *venom* might ultimately derive its name from the Roman goddess of love, Venus. If that's the case, it wouldn't have originally been a poison, but rather a love potion, or some similar concoction brewed up in Venus's name in an attempt to encourage romance.

One question remains, however – where does the modern distinction between *poisons* and *venoms* come from? Well, by the time *venom* arrived in English in the early thirteenth century, it had come to be particularly associated with snakes, while *poisons* had maintained their associations with potions and draughts that had to be ingested in order to have their effect. Although the two continued to cross paths over the years, and are still used all but synonymously today, this early discrepancy seems to have led to the slight distinction in meaning we have today.

*V*olatile

originally meant 'capable of flight'

As well as being used in more general terms to mean 'unpredictable' or 'hot-tempered', today the word *volatile* is often found in relation to chemicals and compounds, including many household products like glues and nail polish removers, that have a high level of 'volatility' – in other words, they readily give off often dangerous vapours. But on its first appearance in the language the word *volatile* was a noun, not an adjective, and had nothing at all to do with poisonous vapours and dangerous chemicals. Far from it in fact – as a *volatile* was originally a winged creature:

As to the volatiles of this country, there are turkeys, pintadoes, parrots, woodquists, turtles, birds of prey, eagles, geese, ducks, herons, white sparrows, tonatzuli, a kind of bird that sings as sweetly as the nightingale, and is of an excellent plumage; and abundance of other birds commonly seen near rivers and forests, quite different from those that are seen in other parts of the world.

— Charles de Rochefort, *The History of the Carriby-Islands* (transl. 1666)

The word *volatile* derives from the Latin word *volare*, meaning 'to fly' (which oddly makes it a distant cousin of *volley* and *volleyball*). From there, an adjective *volatilis* emerged, which not only meant 'winged' or 'capable of flight', but also 'swift', 'fleeting' and, ultimately, 'transitory'. But of all these meanings, it was the winged one that was the first to appear in English and as far back as the early fourteenth century *volatile* was being used as a general name to refer to anything and everything from birds to butterflies. Remarkably this remained the word's only meaning for the next 200 years, and continued to be used right through to the late nineteenth century. Around the early 1600s, however, things began to change.

Although *volatile* maintained its association with flight (as an adjective meaning 'capable of flight' it appeared in the mid 1620s), a number of more figurative uses began to emerge in the seventeenth century. *Volatile* chemicals, with their 'flighty' tendency to vaporise at low temperatures, were first described in a scientific paper in 1605. Soon afterwards, fickle, erratic individuals with ever-changing opinions and interests began to be described as *volatile*, as did anything temporary or difficult to pin down, and as time went by the word continued to develop other connotations of flippancy and levity, hot-headedness and short-temperedness, and eventually unpredictability and impulsiveness.

By the late nineteenth century, these kinds of meanings had all but replaced the earlier literal association between *volatility* and flight. As the word ceased to be used as a noun, the adjectival sense took over and the word has remained synonymous with unpredictability and explosiveness ever since.

Zombie

*was originally a part of a soul
that could be removed by black magic*

'Zombies', according to *Night of the Living Dead* director George A. Romero, 'are the blue-collar monsters.' Ordinary people transformed into extraordinary things. The success of Romero's hugely popular horror films is seen as almost single-handedly establishing the modern image of a mindless, undead, flesh-eating monster in our minds – but the original zombies were nothing of the sort.

The earliest known record of a *zombie* in English dates back to 1819, when the Poet Laureate Robert Southey described a group of escaped slaves who had established a home near Pernambuco, in eastern Brazil:

> They were under the government of an elective Chief, who was chosen for his justice as well as his valour, and held the office for life . . . he was obeyed with perfect loyalty . . . Perhaps a feeling of religion contributed to this obedience; for Zombi, the title whereby he was called, is the name for the Deity in the Angolan tongue.
> – Robert Southey, *History of Brazil, Vol. III* (1819)

Southey was correct in tracing the word *zombie* back to west Africa, and the word is now known to be related to the words *zumbi*, meaning 'fetish' (in its original sense of 'amulet'), and *nzambi*, meaning 'god', in the local Kikongo language. These words were brought to the Americas by the slave trade, ahead of Southey and others discovering them in the early nineteenth century. But while the word came to be used as a title of respect in Brazil, further north things were heading in a very different direction.

In the Caribbean, a voodoo culture mixing traditional African beliefs with elements of western religion was beginning to emerge amongst the slaves and here *zombie* gained a number of different meanings, each referring to some manner of witchcraft or sorcery. According to some accounts, a *zombie* was merely a ghost, particularly a malevolent or malicious one, responsible for causing mishaps and misfortune. According to others, *zombie* became the name of a boogieman figure, 'a phantom . . . not unfrequently heard in the Southern States in nurseries and among the servants', according to an 1872 dictionary of *English of the New World*. And, most sinister of all, in traditional Haitian voodoo a *zombie astral* was the name of a part of a person's soul that could be removed by a local sorcerer or *bokor* and stored in a glass bottle to be traded, held ransom or destroyed. The luckless victim of the bokor's magic would not die, but merely continue to live a half-life, unable to rest until their soul is returned to them.

Precisely which of these meanings was the first to emerge is unclear, but by the early 1900s voodoo culture had begun to infiltrate American popular culture – and had brought these supernatural zombies with it. In 1929, the US journalist William Seabrook published *The Magic Island*, a sensationalised account of Haitian voodoo:

The zombie, they say, is a soulless human corpse, still dead, but taken from the grave and endowed by sorcery with a mechanical semblance of life — it is a dead body which is made to walk and act and move as if it were alive.

Seabrook's account then inspired a film, *White Zombie* (1932), that depicted hordes of zombies as resurrected corpses in the service of a magical sorcerer. Further films and horror stories continued to build on the image of the reanimated dead, until finally Romero's *Night of the Living Dead* (1968) established the flesh-eating zombies we know today.

BIBLIOGRAPHY

Ayto, John. *Dictionary of Word Origins*. New York, 2001.

Bailey, Nathaniel. *An Universal Etymological English Dictionary*. London, 1749.

Barnhart, Robert K. (Ed.) *Barnhart Dictionary of Etymology*. New York, 1988.

Brewer, E. Cobham. *Dictionary of Phrase and Fable*. Philadelphia, 1887.

Cockeram, Henry. *The English Dictionary: An Interpreter of Hard English Words*. London, 1623.

Cresswell, Julia. *Oxford Dictionary of Word Origins* (2nd Ed.) Oxford, 2009.

Crystal, Ben, and David Crystal. *Shakespeare's Words: A Glossary and Language Companion*. London, 2004.

Donald, James. *Chambers's Etymological Dictionary of the English Language*. London, 1877.

Donkin, T. C. *An Etymological Dictionary of the Romance Languages*. Edinburgh, 1864.

Grant, William. *The Scottish National Dictionary*. Edinburgh, 1931–41.

Green, Jonathon. *Chambers Slang Dictionary*. London, 2008.

Grose, Francis. *A Classical Dictionary of the Vulgar Tongue*. London, 1785.

Grose, Francis. *A Glossary of Provincial and Local Words Used in England*. London, 1787.

Halliwell, James. *A Dictionary of Archaic and Provincial Words.* London, 1855.

Jamieson, John. *An Etymological Dicionary of the Scottish Language.* Paisley, 1879.

Johnson, Samuel. *A Dictionary of the English Language.* London, 1755.

Klein, Ernest. *A Comprehensive Etymological Dictionary of the English Language.* Amsterdam, 1971.

Liberman, Anatoly. *Analytic Dictionary of English Etymology.* Minneapolis, 2008.

Nares, Robert. *A Glossary or Collection of Words, Phrases, Names, and Allusions [...] in the Works of English Authors, Particularly Shakespeare, and his Contemporaries.* London, 1859.

Onions, C. T. *A Shakespeare Glossary.* Oxford, 1911.

Partridge, Eric. *A Dictionary of Slang and Unconventional English* (8th Ed.) London, 1984.

Partridge, Eric. *The Routledge Dictionary of Historical Slang* (Revised 6th Ed.) London, 1973.

Skeat, Walter. *A Glossary of Tudor and Stuart Words.* Oxford, 1914.

Wedgwood, Hensleigh. *A Dictionary of English Etymology.* New York, 1878.

Weekley, Ernest. *An Etymological Dictionary of Modern English.* London, 1921.

Wright, Joseph. *The English Dialect Dictionary (Vols. 1–6).* Oxford, 1896–1905.

Wright, Thomas. *Dictionary of Obsolete and Provincial Words.* London, 1857.